THE BRACERO EXPERIENCE

Elitelore versus Folklore

A Book on Lore

UCLA LATIN AMERICAN STUDIES

Volume 43

THE
Bracero
Experience
Elitelore
versus Folklore

María Herrera-Sobek

with an Introduction by

James W. Wilkie

UCLA LATIN AMERICAN CENTER PUBLICATIONS

University of California, Los Angeles

UCLA Latin American Center

University of California, Los Angeles

Copyright © 1979 by The Regents of the University of California

ISBN: 0-87903-043-7

Library of Congress Catalog Number: 78-620046

Printed in the United States of America

Grateful acknowledgment is made to the following to whom all rights are reserved:

Indiana University Press, Bloomington, Indiana, for the corridos from Merle E. Simmons, *The Mexican Corrido as a Source for Interpretative Study of Modern Mexico (1870–1950)*.

The Instituto de Investigaciones Estéticas, Universidad Nacional Autónoma de México, for "De 'El interior' o 'Los enganchados,' " "Del viaje de la 'Típica de Policía' a California," "De 'La maquinita' o de 'El emigrante,' " "De 'El traque' o de 'El lava-platos.' "

Songs of Mexico, Inc., New York, for "Chulas Fronteras" and "Natalio Reyes Colás."

Grever International, S.A., for "Cruzando el puente" and "El corrido de los mojados."

Ediciones Musicales Rimo, S.A., for "Los alambrados."

Golden Sands Enterprises, Inc., for "Juan Mojao," "Uno más de los mojados," "Lamento de un bracero," "La descriminación."

Revista Chicano-Riqueña for "Corrido de los desarraigados."

Francisco García for "El corrido del ilegal."

Photo facing title page: United Press International Photo

Proceeds from the sale of this publication are being used to match funds from the National Endowment for the Humanities Challenge Grant No. CE-31990-78-971, to the University of California, Los Angeles.

To my grandfather
JOSÉ PABLO TARANGO
a bracero from the Hacienda de San Miguel
Valparaíso, Zacatecas

Contents

Preface

This study analyzes the elitelore of various Mexican authors as exhibited in fictional works about the experiences in the United States of Mexican braceros—documented or undocumented temporary workers. This elitelore is tested in relation to folklore in two ways: oral history interviews with braceros and examination of bracero folk songs.

The term "elitelore," originated by James W. Wilkie, is defined as that body of knowledge which includes self-perception about the organization of ideas on personal and group past and about the building of myths. It also includes the self-deception necessary for the protection of the self-image of political or intellectual leaders and of nations in their struggle with complexities that they only partly understand. Although leaders do not admit to having a lore, they betray it in their political speeches and it is recognizable in their fiction. A salient aspect of the elitelore of literary writers is that their works influence society at large, often helping to formulate government policy and to change, for better or for worse, the self-perception of a society as a whole.

Written elitelore can function positively and negatively in a society; an author can influence, to a certain extent, the self-image of a society. For example, it is not uncommon in primitive societies for bards or poets to extol the divine origins of a group or tribe. A more recent example of elitelore wherein a nation's positive self-image was created is the settling of the West in the United States. Americans are inundated with popular literature, movies, books, and paintings that depict hardy pioneers of the nineteenth century conquering the West.

In contrast with the positive self-image of these American immigrants, their Mexican counterparts of the same region in the twentieth century have suffered from an elitelore promulgated in fiction written during the 1940s and 1950s by Mexican intellectuals wishing to expose maltreatment of Mexican immigrants in the United States. To defend the human rights of Mexican immigrant workers, the bracero immigration was generally treated in the literature as a despicable experience. The main thrust of such works was to level criticism at the governments of Mexico and the United States, the former for its failure to live up to the promises of the Revolution of 1910, the latter for allowing the exploitation of poor Mexicans. The promises of the Revolution to provide land and an adequate standard of living failed to materialize for many reasons, two being the exploding birth rate and the dramatic drop in infant mortality. Disappointment and embarrassment of Mexican writers coupled with the desire of Mexican government officials to divert attention from their failures helped forge the image of a downtrodden Mexican worker.

That the bracero was not the main focus of the protest is evidenced by the fact that no true bracero hero appeared in the literary works. The bracero was used mainly as a tool to protest the government policies of both Mexico and the United States. As a matter of fact, the bracero himself was criticized—both explicitly and implicitly—for daring to show the world that Mexico was starving. In *Tenemos sed* by Magdalena Mondragón (1956) the Mexican immigrant is depicted explicitly as a greedy scoundrel who got what he deserved—suffering and exploitation in the United States. In *Aventuras de un bracero* a biographical novel by Jesus Topete (1949), the Mexican worker who stayed in the United States and became a United States citizen is attacked even more virulently. The negative portrayal of these human beings implies that anyone of Mexican descent who goes to the United States and stays becomes a despicable character not to be emulated. It is a warning to other braceros: "If you stay in the United States you will become like him—a fate worse than death," as illustrated in the following passage from Topete's novel:

With respect to those types of creatures [Mexican Americans or Chicanos] I had a few facts. There had been two of them in the camp when we came. There was one that had been living in the United States for more than forty years and who had become a naturalized citizen. He did not have any family. He used to talk about the horrors of Mexico and the Mexicans whom he characterized as a bunch of poverty-stricken dirty people. The other one was a real *pocho,*[1] born in the United States of

[1]*Pocho, -cha.,* m. and f. 1. "Word used to designate those North Americans of Spanish origin, especially those of Mexican origin. It is used in the southern part of the United States, particularly in California, also applied to Mexicans or Spanish citizens residing in the United States. (In Mexico, *poche* and *pocha* are more commonly used. It probably has the same origin as *pochie,* a word native to Sonora, Mexico, and probably comes from the Yaqui language. It also has the meaning of being limited in intelligence, more bluntly, stupid.) 2. Corrupted Castilian. Mixture of bad English and terrible Spanish that is spoken by the North American residents of Spanish origin, mainly Mexicans in California (United States)." See *Diccionario General de Americanismos* (1942), Pedro Robredo.

Mexican parents. He was a sneaky, hypocritical bootlicker and a cheat who picked clean many of my friends. He would invite some of the braceros to go out to drink so that they would pay for his drinks. Finally they caught him stealing from one of our countryman braceros whom he had gotten drunk. . . . (pp. 50-52).

That the negative image projected by Mexican writers has had a deleterious effect on the self-image of the Chicano is noticeable in the lack of strong, powerful heroic figures of epic proportion in Chicano literature dealing with Mexican immigration. The image of a hero of mythic proportions has yet to materialize in Chicano fiction. Current images of main protagonists portrayed in outstanding Chicano fiction include a child in Rudolfo Anaya's *Bless Me Ultima* (1972); a raunchy antihero in Oscar Acosta's *The Revolt of the Cockroach People* (1973), and the hesitant, unsure protagonist of Jose Antonio Villarreal's *Pocho* (1959). The image of the downtrodden Mexican worker has been etched into the subconscious mind of the Chicano, and, solidly crystallized, it is difficult to erase. With literature and the mass media constantly pounding into the consciousness of the Chicano the image of a pathetic, weak, easily exploited Mexican, it is now difficult to conceptualize the bracero or Mexican immigrant in any other terms. This image has particularly corrosive effects on the minds of young Chicano children and adolescents who frequently refer to anything Mexican as "wetback" or "T.J. stuff" and do not want to be associated with it.

The lore of the Mexican literary elite about the bracero, whether written with good intentions or not, has been detrimental to the Chicano. Many people in Mexico, no doubt influenced by this negative lore, many times treat the Chicano at best with pity and in a condescending manner, at worst with scorn. The image may be defined as that of a man unable to control his destiny; a man at the mercy of an unfeeling, uncaring universe and exploitative society. Since this image has been common for a quarter of a century and is one that is readily acceptable to most people, it probably bears some truth, but how much is open to question.

I conducted my study as an experiment to test the extent to which images presented in the news media, books, and magazines correspond to the image the bracero has of himself. I compared the literary works of Mexican fiction writers with the actual experiences and folk songs of braceros. This was done because, on cursory analysis of the literary works, a definite body of elitelore related to the bracero experience was discernible. An interesting contrast, therefore, can be made between the different authors' elitelore, as evidenced in their writings, and the folklore held by the bracero, as evidenced in oral interviews with them and in *corridos* and other folk songs.

The term "folklore" in this study includes both oral and written forms of lore. Oral interviews yield excellent vehicles by which we can examine the beliefs, traditions, customs, legends, and myths of self held by the folk. Although unwritten, the interview provides substantial information on how a particular phenomenon is perceived and how the lore resulting from the perception of the phenomenon influences the actions and worldview of the folk. Through the oral lore of the folk, information, whether true or false, is transmitted from one segment of the population to another. Eventually a more formalized and structured form of lore appears as perceived in the jokes about Mexican immigrants and in folk songs, particularly the corrido.

I examine the oral interview and the corrido together with other types of folk songs as two forms of folklore reflecting the attitudes of the folk toward the particular phenomenon of Mexican immigration to the United States.

Dictionary, common usage, and legal meaning of the term "bracero" do not always agree. The Zerolo and Toro y Gómez *Diccionario de la Lengua Castellana* (1911) defines the bracero as "Peon who is hired to dig or do any other type of farm work." In current usage the term is applied to any male Mexican who has gone to work in the agricultural fields of the United States. In legal terms it has come to mean a male laborer who is legally contracted from the Mexican government by the United States government to work for American farmers.

The bracero's predecessors were the Chinese, first employed in the railroads and mines and later in agriculture, and then the Japanese who were imported into the United States as laborers during the third quarter of the nineteenth century. As the Chinese workers flourished, resentment and racial prejudice against them increased. Congress ended this immigration in 1882 with the passage of the Chinese Exclusion Act. The Japanese who followed proved to be highly experienced, hardworking and frugal farmers who soon bought land and established themselves as farmers. This was not viewed with approval by native American farmers and the importation of Japanese laborers ceased in 1907 with the "Gentlemen's Agreement" between Japan and the United States (Galarza, 1964:34).

World War I brought with it a shortage of labor to the United States. Under provisions of the 1917 Immigration Act, Mexicans were imported to help meet the labor shortage that had developed as a result of the war. At the end of World War I, Mexicans were replaced by Filipinos from the Hawaiian Islands.

During World War II another manpower shortage ensued owing to industry's heavy recruitment and the military draft. To relieve this manpower shortage, the Mexican peasant was called upon. On August 4, 1942, an agreement was drawn up between Mexico and the United States initiating a government-regulated migration of braceros on a large scale. The agreement stated (United States Executive Agreement Series 278, 1943:3):

1. Mexican laborers shall not be subject to the military draft.
2. Discrimination against braceros is forbidden.
3. They shall be guaranteed transportation, food, hospitalization and repatriation.
4. They shall not be used to displace other workers nor to lower wages.
5. Contracts made by employee and employer will be made under the supervision of the Mexican government and shall be written in Spanish.
6. Expenses incurred for transportation and lodgings from point of origin to destination shall be paid by the employer who will be reimbursed by sub-employer.

With regard to work and salary, the principal points were:

1. Salaries shall be the same as those made to citizens of the U.S.A. and shall not be lower than 30 cents an hour.
2. Exceptions as to wages can be made under extenuating circumstances provided authorization by the Mexican government is given.
3. No minors under 14 will be allowed to work.
4. Braceros will be allowed to form associations and elect a leader to represent them.
5. They shall be guaranteed work for 75 percent of the working days.
6. Savings shall be deducted from their pay and the Banco Nacional Agrícola shall take charge of the money until the braceros return.

The commission that drafted the agreement was composed of representatives from Mexico and the United States. Those from Mexico were E. Hidalgo, Chief Official representing the Secretary of Exterior Relations, and Abraham J. Nava, a Representative of the Work and Social Welfare Department. The United States representatives included John O. Walker, Sub-Administrator for the Farm Security Administration under the Department of Agriculture, and David Meeker, Sub-Director of the Office of Agricultural Relations of War and Department of Agriculture.

These provisions, although revised several times, were kept essentially the same and incorporated in 1951 into U.S. Public

'Law 78, which governed the program until it was officially ter-
minated on December 31, 1964, when Congress failed to extend
the statute regulating the bracero program ("Migratory Farm
Labor" 1965:634–635).

The process of recruitment used between 1951 and 1964 differed
according to whether or not the bracero was "certified" or "free."
A bracero sought to be certified by the mayor of his town, who
vouched for the bracero's character and need of employment. The
certified bracero then proceeded to a recruiting center at either
Empalme, Chihuahua, or Monterrey, where he waited to be called
for transfer to the United States. Free braceros, those who could
not or did not obtain certificates, simply went to the recruiting
centers hoping to be called for transfer anyway—free braceros
formed three-quarters of all recruits going to the United States.

When the bracero was chosen, he was vaccinated, fingerprinted,
given a physical examination, loaded on a bus, and taken to a
U.S. reception center. There he was X-rayed, dusted with
D.D.T., and again given a thorough physical examination. Here
the contracts were read and jobs offered. Wages ranked from 60
cents to $1.25 per hour. The bracero had five days to make up his
mind as to which contract he wished to accept. Contracts varied in
duration, the average being for about three months.

Although the bracero program ended in 1964, Mexicans have
continued to cross the border into the United States and to work
with and without documents or legal status. Many of today's
"undocumented workers" continue to move back and forth across
the U.S.-Mexican border enjoying and suffering many of the same
experiences treated here.

ACKNOWLEDGMENTS

This work would not have been possible had I not obtained a
UCLA International Comparative Studies grant from the Ford
Foundation during the summer of 1969 while a graduate student
in the Latin American Studies Program at the University of California, Los Angeles. I would like to thank Johannes Wilbert,
Director of the UCLA Latin American Center, for the support I
received in carrying out this study.

I particularly want to express my sincere thanks and apprecia-
tion to James W. Wilkie for all the suggestions, ideas, and time he

has contributed to this project. It was Professor Wilkie from the start who guided me and inspired me to write the original master's thesis from which this work later developed. It was also Professor Wilkie and his wife Edna Monzón de Wilkie who spent many hours editing and reading the different drafts of this book. I gratefully acknowledge their help.

Of course I will always remember the people of Huecorio for whom I developed a great love and respect. I thank them for making my stay in Huecorio a most unforgettable experience.

A note of thanks is also in order to my thesis advisor John A. Crow, UCLA Spanish and Portuguese Department, and to Cynthia Norte for typing the final manuscript.

Finally I want to thank my husband Joseph and my son Erik Jason for their encouragement.

Introduction

by

JAMES W. WILKIE

In this volume María Herrera-Sobek reorients our understanding of bracero life, advances methodology in oral history, and demonstrates the interplay of elitelore and folklore. She examines Mexican novels and describes the view of that country's literary elite of the folk experience of Mexico's farm laborers, or braceros, who temporarily migrate to the United States. By means of tape-recorded interviews with braceros about their own experiences, she develops a unique methodology of oral history investigation. The viewpoint of a composite bracero is created by synthesizing the experiences of the many into one, an artistic innovation based upon social science research. Finally, she tests the elitelore of the novels and the folklore of the interviews against the images drawn by the braceros in their own folk songs, or corridos.

The new field of elitelore is based upon the tenet that the lore of leaders can undergo the same kind of analysis that the lore of followers receives in the field of folklore. The elite may have resisted this idea in the past, perhaps subconsciously, under a misapprehension that they alone have access to the truth, deeming the rest of the people, the folk, unable or unwilling to comprehend complex events and issues. It sometimes comes as a shock to the elite to find their own "truths" may be studied as aspects of lore, and they feel threatened that they can be studied or examined in the same way that the folk have been by them, that their thoughts and elite ways can be disected and analyzed. Not until recently have scholars begun to investigate the views of leaders as explicitly "lore."[1]

Lore connotes personal "wisdom" gained through accumulated life experiences and includes the building of myths and deceptions

---

[1] For the basic statement, see James W. Wilkie, *Elitelore* (Los Angeles: UCLA Latin American Center Publications, 1973), pp. 9–10, 61–65.

1

of self to justify one's situation in life. The elite construct personal lore to shield the ego from self-doubt that would hamper their leadership. The folk use personal lore to explain and rationalize the predicaments in which they find themselves, as exemplified in sayings and songs that help followers through life and minimize the need to question too closely where they are being led.

Lore clearly is not class-oriented. The elite express their lore at all levels of society: for example, congressmen are the political elites seen at the national level, councilmen at the local level, and wisemen at the tribal level. On this continuum from national to tribal level folk knowledge is shared by leaders (elite) and followers (folk) alike, the difference between these residing in the special "knowledge" possessed by the former become ever more sophisticated the higher the place on the political ladder. That is not to say that leaders act outside the course of forces such as changes in institutions or in long-term economic cycles. Rather, the elite interpret the meaning of change and offer leadership for comprehending and resolving at all levels of society the stress generated when continuity is interrupted and life situations are changed.

María Herrera-Sobek shows how the Mexican literary elite interpret the meaning of the bracero migration from Mexico to the United States. The writers did not participate in the experience but their generally negative explanation of it has come to be very influential, eventually tending to overcome positive Mexican folk perceptions of the same migration. Because of the power of elite writers to influence non-braceros in Mexico and in the United States, the self-image of braceros gradually came to include the impression of themselves as seen in novels. Although Mexico's novelists thought that they were right in protecting Mexico from the loss of some of its best labor (and at the same time protecting Mexican laborers from exploitation), in reality they tended indirectly to help convince the bracero of his inferiority.

The many braceros who remained in the United States instead of returning to Mexico then found themselves culturally adrift and without a positive image to explain what was happening to them as they became part Mexican, part American. Earlier waves of migrants from Mexico chose to call themselves Mexican-Americans, seeking to identify with and, in the end, become "one hundred percent American." Not until the successful advent of the Chicano movement in the United States in the 1960s was the idea of the innate inferiority of Mexican-Americans seriously questioned. It was the younger generation who sought to overcome the stereotypes encouraged by Mexican novelists who were in their own way well meaning but unaware of the impact that their works would have on families many of whose members would move back and forth across the border almost at will or would not return to Mexico at all.

Mexican novelists cannot alone be blamed for the negative image of the Mexican worker. In farming regions U.S. citizens have been prone to look askance at "foreigners," and Mexico's poor workers who did not speak English would have had a difficult time in maintaining self-pride even if they had not been abandoned by a strategic elite who might have helped their self-image instead of hindering it. It took the Chicanos themselves, many being the sons and daughters of braceros, to build a new image, a new lore, that would give their people importance in their new homeland.

María Herrera-Sobek, granddaughter of a bracero from Zacatecas, arrived at the University of California, Los Angeles, in the late 1960s with a desire to investigate her past, an endeavor that Chicanos were beginning to undertake at that particular time. Bright and earnest, she had made her way through Arizona State University in spite of financial problems and heavy obligations to her extended family. Although she had received her B.A. in chemistry with distinction in 1965, at UCLA she entered Latin American Studies with the goal of doing research in Mexico. The idea intrigued her of utilizing oral history interviews to create the life story of a composite bracero which could be tested against the novelist's view of the bracero, and she at once set about making that vague idea a concrete reality. An obvious choice as the site of her research was the village of Huecorio in the state of Michoacán, Mexico. It was the only Mexican community studied in fully economic terms, and it had revealed that more than half the economically employed males had at one time or another been a bracero.[2] She went to Mexico in 1969 to conduct her interviews but transcription was delayed when she had to devote time to the illness of her grandfather. Then she reappeared in Los Angeles with hundreds of pages of transcribed oral interviews, the nucleus of her Master's thesis in Latin American Studies which she completed in 1971 under Professors John Crow (Department of Spanish), Johannes Wilbert (Department of Anthropology), and myself (Department of History). Advancing to the doctorate, which she received in 1975 from the UCLA Department of Spanish and Portuguese, she maintained her interest in the problem of elitelore and folklore.

[2] See Michael Belshaw, *A Village Economy: Land and People of Huecorio* (New York: Columbia University Press, 1967).

Undeterred by teaching, marriage, and motherhood, she began to study the bracero folk song in order to revise her Master's thesis for publication. After collecting and translating most of the sixteen folk songs analyzed here, her research efforts again proved fruitful, the bracero image in song tending to reinforce the results of her oral interviews in Huecorio.

María Herrera-Sobek's contribution to oral history falls into an interesting scholarly context beginning with the early research of Manuel Gamio and continuing in other forms to the recent work of such scholars as Robert Redfield, Jorge Bustamante, Oscar Lewis, Julian Samora and Eugene Nelson. During 1926 and 1927 Manuel Gamio carried out research on Mexican immigration to the United States by interviewing seventy-two persons who had moved north and four persons of Mexican descent born in the United States. Some of the immigrants were interviewed on their way back to Mexico, some had settled in the United States, and some were moving back and forth depending upon job and family prospects. For these interviews Gamio developed a guide for fieldworkers in the form of "An Outline of Points to be Considered, Both Objectively and Subjectively." The guide covered questions about life history keyed to the following items: birth, birth control, marriage and death ceremonies, food, housing, clothing, religion, amusements, sports, work, economic situation, education, vices, crimes, race prejudice, patriotism, affiliations, superstition, and attitude toward American life. From these interviews he extracted his analysis published in 1930.[3] The interviews themselves, generally written down after the fact, were not published.

Robert Redfield saw the value of the Gamio interviews, however, and he selected portions of them for publication in 1931 under the following topics: the Mexican leaves home, first contacts, the United States as a base for revolutionary activity, economic adjustment, conflict and race-consciousness, the leader and the intellectual, assimilation, and the Mexican-American. By breaking down the Gamio interviews according to topic, the Redfield approach meant that the result did not give "life history" as suggested in the title, *The Mexican Immigrant: His Life-Story.*[4] Thus, particular individuals could only be followed according to topics and no one could be followed according to successive life history

[3]Manuel Gamio, *Mexican Immigration to the United States; A Study of Human Migration and Adjustment* (Chicago: University of Chicago Press, 1930; repr. Arno Press and The New York Times, 1969).

[4]Chicago: University of Chicago Press, 1931. Republished as *The Life of the Mexican Immigrant: Autobiographical Documents Collected by Manuel Gamio* (New York: Dover, 1971).

events, much having been left out as not fitting within the topics selected.

From another point of view, Redfield himself was aware of a problem with the title *Mexican Immigrant: His Life-Story.* In the preface he wrote that the Gamio interviews did not illustrate the "life history technique" as understood by sociologists because Gamio's documents represent brief statements made to hurried investigators in the course of casual contacts. According to Redfield, if Gamio had used the life history technique he would have delved into past experiences in order to develop as complete a picture as possible of the successive events in each individual's life. The resulting subjective autobiographic statement of the subject's career (developed in a long study by the investigator and obtained only after suitable rapport had been established) would have been tested against outside objective views.

If Redfield noted that not all the contents of Gamio's accounts were of equal worth because interviews yield a person's rationalized view of situations, he also recognized that it is just these viewpoints and rationalizations that become the scientific data. "Rationalizations," he wrote, "are useful in explaining and anticipating conduct because people act, not only because things are so, but because they think them, or assume them, to be so."[5]

In the sense of recording life experiences, then, Gamio's work and Redfield's presentation of it anticipated Herrera-Sobek's research. But where Herrera-Sobek portrays the Mexican worker as having optimistic attitudes, Gamio found pessimistic attitudes revealing stark views of life indeed. Redfield summarized Gamio's oral documents as follows:

The experiences of the Mexican of little education . . . repeat themselves almost to monotony: the insecurity or unrest in Mexico, the feeling of helplessness in the new country, the little organization of the immigrant community, the mobility and isolation, the security following upon satisfactory economic adjustment, the reflective or resentful attitude attendant upon insight gained into the ways and prejudices of Americans. Not all these features are present in all the documents, but several of them are in most cases. A generalization is, therefore, built up by a mental procedure hard to describe adequately.[6]

---

[5]Ibid., pp. xii–xiii. For broad theory of and method for obtaining life histories, see Jorge Balán, ed., *Las Historias de Vida en Ciencias Sociales; Teoría y Técnica* (Buenos Aires: Nueva Visión, 1974). For specialized practice in a statistical case study of internal migration, cf. Jorge Balán, Harley Browning, and Elizabeth Jelin, *Men in a Developing Society: Geography and Social Mobility in Monterrey, Mexico* (Austin: University of Texas Press, 1973).

[6]Ibid., p. xiv.

In this manner, Redfield noted, the reader comes to know no particular pre-1930 Mexican immigrant but a sort of generalized one.

In the category "the leader and the intellectual," Gamio set down the following thoughts of Pascual Tejeda, a U.S. university graduate and a former Mexican consul, who remarked that he had studied "American life" in all of its aspects and accordingly was "not afraid" to say that he liked the United States a great deal. About immigration he concluded:

The Mexican immigrants do not adapt themselves to modern American life on account of their lack of culture. . . . [But] the humiliations, the prejudice and the lack of esteem which are shown toward the Mexican race here are also due to the great lack of culture of the American people.

The immigration of Mexicans to the United States does not benefit either Mexico in general nor the Mexicans in particular. In the first place because of their lack of education the Mexican peons do not adapt themselves to the customs of this country but on the contrary learn everything bad and that is what they take back on their return. Here they are made victims of all kinds of exploitation and they are humiliated. It also happens that the majority of the immigrants who come remain here even when they go back for a while to Mexico. Many of these immigrants who didn't even know what a bed was in our country learn to know what it is as well as many other things. But that doesn't make for progress for so much energy goes out of Mexico when what our country needs most is working men.[7]

Although mistreatment of Mexicans entering the United States illegally has continued into the 1970s, Jorge Bustamente could write of his participant-observer's experience as a "wetback" for the University of Notre Dame U.S.-Mexico Border Studies Project by noting that he had been protected by U.S. Border Patrol officers to whom he had been turned over by Texas ranchhands who had captured him soon after crossing the border. Bustamente recounts his capture by the ranchhands as follows:

[We] were going up a little hill from the top of which Juan wanted to check our location when we saw a jeep coming in our direction. It appeared so suddenly that we did not have time to hide ourselves. We stood still, looking at the jeep, which stopped about sixty feet from us. Three people got out and pointed their rifles at us. Our reaction was to get down on the ground; then they began to shoot. After the first shots it was obvious that they did not want to kill us but they kept on shooting

[7]Ibid., p. 185. It is noteworthy that Tejeda himself did not choose to return to Mexico because of political turmoil and job insecurity.

and all the while we could hear them laughing and shouting. One of the bullets must have hit very close to me because I felt little pieces of dirt hitting my head.

They stopped shooting and came to us, laughing and insulting us in English. One of them told Juan something like, "Get up, you greaser, you are not dead."

We stood up and one of them asked me in very broken Spanish if I knew what "No Trespassing" meant; I said I did not. Then he said in English something like "You damn Mexicans don't know anything about law . . . you only know how to steal, huh?"

Then another said in an angry tone, "You better tell all the 'wets' to stop coming through this ranch." He added in broken Spanish that the next time they would shoot at us to kill.[8]

Yet autobiographical sketches of those braceros who do not get caught in the United States suggest that however difficult life might be, exploitation of them at times is worse in Mexico. Manuel Sánchez expressed this view to Oscar Lewis in oral history interviews published in 1961 as follows:

The *braceros* I knew all agreed on one thing, that the United States was "a toda madre." That means it's the best. Every once in a while someone complained . . . like Alberto said the Texans were lousy sons-of-bitches because they treated Mexicans like dogs. And we looked badly upon the discrimination against the Negroes. . . .

But we all noticed that even the workers who were not so well off had their car and refrigerator. When it came to equality and standard of living, well, they'd lynch me for saying this, but I believe that the United States is practically communistic . . . within capitalism, that is. At least it was in California, because I even heard a worker shout at his boss, and the boss just shut up. The workers there are protected in lots of ways. Here in Mexico, the bosses are tyrants.

Thinking of Mexico's system of life, I am very disappointed. It is just that when I was living in the United States, I could see that people were glad when a friend got ahead, you know what I mean? "Congratulations, man, it's great that things are going good with you." Everybody would congratulate him if he bought a new car or a house or something. But in Mexico, when a friend of mine, with a lot of sacrifice and hard work and skimping on food, finally managed to buy a new delivery truck, what happened? He parked it in front of his house and when he came out all the paint was scratched off. If that isn't pure envy, what is it?

Instead of trying to raise a person's morale, our motto here is, "If I am a worm, I'm going to make the next fellow feel like a louse." Yes, here you always have to feel you are above. I have felt this way myself, that's why I say it. I guess I'm a Mexican, all right. Even if you live on

[8]From Julian Samora, *Los Mojados: The Wetback Story* (Notre Dame, Ind.: University of Notre Dame Press, 1971), p. 119.

the bottom level, you have to feel higher up. I've seen it among the trash pickers; there's rank even among thieves. They start arguing, "You so-and-so, all you steal is old shoes. But me, when I rob, I rob good stuff." So the other one says, "You! Turpentine is all you drink. At least, I knock off my 96-proof pure alcohol, which is more than you ever do." That's the way things are here.[9]

That Manuel Sánchez may have been overly impressed with bracero life is suggested in Eugene Nelson's *Pablo Cruz and the American Dream,* the most comprehensive autobiographical account of a single bracero yet published. In the introduction to *Pablo Cruz,* Julian Samora sums up the story in the following terms:

This story, like so many similar ones, begins in a village in Mexico and ends in a metropolis in the United States. This is a story of "success"; most are not.

Success here is not measured in the attainment of high status, or prestige, or power. Rather, it is keeping warm at night, avoiding the *Migra* (Immigration and Naturalization Service), having something to eat, getting a miserable temporary job, entering the society legally, and maintaining a personal integrity and dignity. For these seemingly small rewards, the price in physical and psychological suffering is high.[10]

Taking a different approach to summarize the bracero experience, María Herrera-Sobek here creates the story of a composite bracero. By selecting villagers from different socioeconomic neighborhoods of Huecorio and by choosing braceros who migrated in different epochs since 1947, she attempts to give us a new method for obtaining representative analysis.

Even with advances in oral history methodology in this volume, however, readers may question the degree to which valid conclusions may be drawn from viewpoints tape-recorded in only one of the thousands of small Mexican villages from which the bracero has come. If it is obvious that caution must be used in generalizing from the Huecorio experience, it is also apparent that the composite account presented here is more representative than any published account to date. Gamio's interviews may have covered a wider array of topics, but Redfield published only parts of his interviews. By testing the interviews against the novelists' view, we

---

[9]Oscar Lewis, *The Children of Sánchez: Autobiography of a Mexican Family* (New York: Random House, 1961), pp. 338–339. On the theory of "limited good" exemplified here in the words of Manuel Sánchez, see George M. Foster, *Tzintzuntan: Mexican Peasants in a Changing World* (Boston: Little, Brown, 1967), chapter 6.

[10]In Eugene Nelson, *Pablo Cruz and the American Dream* (Layton, Utah: Peregrine Smith, 1975), second page of unpaginated Introduction.

can see that the lore of the Mexican migrant has been influenced by a stereotyped depiction, and that the folk song has been overshadowed by the literary form.

One answer to those who argue, especially in light of the work of Gamio, that the bracero experience has not been as positive as depicted by Herrera-Sobek, is that the author of this book recorded the experiences of migrants who returned to Mexico in the post-1940 era whereas Gamio talked mainly with migrants still in the United States in the pre-1940 era. From the U.S. viewpoint, during the 1920s and 1930s, when the U.S. rural economy was depressed and opportunity for the Mexican migrant declined drastically, the bracero came under severe criticism as having "deprived Americans of jobs." When the United States was at war during the 1940s, 1950s, and 1960s, the bracero gained some status as he replaced U.S. workers sent off to fight. By the 1970s, however, a series of U.S. "rolling recessions" meant that the excess labor supplied by Mexico would again lose status. From the Mexican viewpoint, the Mexican elite generally had considered Mexico to be underpopulated so that the loss of workers was considered to harm the country's development and the bracero was seen to be a "traitor." Economic crisis in Mexico during the 1970s, however, meant that the country's elite would adopt an old idea that migration of workers to the United States was not so much to be condemned as to be seen as a convenient escape valve for excess workers. From Herrera-Sobek's viewpoint, the bracero tends to be a hardworking person who simply looks for work, regardless of national "legal" boundaries.

Part One

ELITELORE

1

The Bracero Experience in Fiction

Down through the ages writers record the events of their times. Many Mexican writers have described in their fiction the bracero experience, and in doing so have covered most of the twentieth century. Some of the novels and short stories examined in this study are of superior literary value; others are poorly written works of social protest which neglect other aspects that produce lasting literature.

In analyzing the fictional works—one drama, four short stories, and seven novels—three basic periods of action can be discerned.

1. The period of the Mexican Revolution (1910-1917)
2. The Depression Years (1930-1935)
3. The aftermath of World War II (1948-1960)

The period of the Mexican Revolution was marked by extreme unrest. Hunger and violence were rampant throughout Mexico; bands of armed men roamed the country fighting Federal soldiers and harshly affecting the lives of the peasants. Hacienda[1] life was completely disrupted and the cities were in constant turmoil. The end result was drastic social upheavals and dislocations. Many villages were abandoned en masse and thousands of individuals migrated to the United States in search of a better life. Some brought their families while others went alone. Although the bracero had begun to make his mark in history, his full emergence did not materialize until the next period.

The second period dealing with the bracero experience began with the Depression. In the early part of this period the influx of Mexicans into the United States continued, but these people found that the United States could not provide enough jobs for its own citizens let alone those of a neighboring country. Mexicans were

---

[1] Mixed agricultural and livestock grazing estate which was considered large by the standards of the region. For a discussion of the colonial land and labor system see Jaime Rodríguez and Colin MacLachlan, *New Spain: An Interpretive History of Colonial Mexico*. Berkeley: University of California Press. Forthcoming.

being sent back to Mexico by the thousands during the Depression years under the Repatriation Program (Hoffman, 1976:83–179). This, coupled with the fact that Mexico as a whole was being reorganized, and postrevolutionary leaders were promising agrarian reform eventually produced an exodus of Mexican braceros who returned or were forcefully sent back to their native country. This period was portrayed by Juan Bustillo Oro in his drama, "Los que vuelven" (1933).

The third and most important period in terms of the number of braceros who went to the United States and the quantity and quality of literature produced dealing with the subject came after World War II. The United States, having engaged itself in a world war, found its fields empty of able-bodied men, and it asked Mexico to fill these fields with men. Having declared war on the Axis, Mexico promised to comply. Consequently, thousands of men, in some years numbering over half a million, filled the American fields with the Spanish language and all the attitudes and customs that characterized their culture. The end result of this program was a tremendous impact on the sociological, economic, and political aspects of American society.

Many important novels dealing with braceros were written during the postwar period, some being historical novels and some dealing with current events. With regard to history, two important works are discussed here: Agustín Yáñez's *The Edge of the Storm* first published in Spanish in 1947 and translated into English in 1963, which described events in 1909, and Rafael F. Múñoz's short story "El repatriado" published in 1960, which described life in 1913. Other works analyzed here belonging to the postwar period are Luis Spota's *Murieron a mitad del río* (1948), J. de Jesús Becerra González's *El dólar viene del norte* (1954), Héctor Raúl Almanza's *Huelga blanca* (1950), Carlos Fuentes's *La región más transparente* (1958), Juan Rulfo's short story "Paso del Norte" (1967), María Luisa Melo de Remes's two short stories: "Brazos que se van" and "Pobre patria mía" both (1955), Jesús Topete's *Aventuras de un bracero* (1949), and Magdalena Mondragón's *Tenemos Sed* (1956).

All these works contain negative aspects of the bracero experience, although the better writers, such as Agustín Yáñez and Carlos Fuentes, present positive aspects, too, often as a function of time of events.

1909

The writings are examined in order of time of the events portrayed. In *The Edge of the Storm,* Agustín Yáñez shows life in a small town of Jalisco in central Mexico right after the turn of the century. This psychologically ill town is presented as being completely closed to outside influences on both thought and action. As the novel opens, the whole ''pueblo'' is ''hermetically closed'' physically and spiritually. The psychological turmoil within each individual and in the town as a whole is brought out and composes the bulk of the novel. One of the principal characters, Damián, a bracero who has lived in the United States and has returned home with new political and spiritual ideas, is depicted by his fellow villagers as follows:

Like plague-laden winds, themselves a plague, worse than the donkey-drivers. (It's hard to say which is worse, their absence or their return . . . To say nothing of the families and fields deserted.)

''It's worse when they come back,'' most people say.

''And they gain nothing from their experience.''

''Even those who come back with money aren't satisfied here any longer.''

''Many of them don't want to work anymore; they just strut around, air their opinions, and criticize everything.''

''They're a bad example, making fun of religion, the country, the customs.''

''They sow doubt, undermine patriotism, and encourage others to leave this 'filthy, poverty-stricken country.' ''

''They're the ones who spread ideas of Masonry, Socialism, and Spiritism.''

''They've no respect for women.''

''Nor sense of obligation at all.''

''They're vicious and quarrelsome, always ready to pick a fight.''

''They've lost the fear of God, that's the sum of it.''

''And there are more and more of them all the time. Nobody gets any peace. They meddle with everything—with the rich for being rich and the poor for being poor. They have no respect for anyone.''

''Miserable people! Poor country!''

''They think because they can roll off a few strange words they know more than anybody else and are a cut above other people, but they can't read a bit better than when they went away.''

''Just because they have some gold teeth and are always ready for a fight.''

''Because they come back with round-toed shoes, felt hats, wide-legged trousers, and shirts with wristbands and shiny cuff-links.''

''With their hair bushy in front and shaved behind.''

''They don't even have a mustache.''

''They're ridiculous.''

''They certainly are. When poor old Don Pedro Rubio's son-in-law came back and saw them stirring *atole,* he said he couldn't remember the word for it!''

"But he remembered how to stir up trouble all right."

"They're ridiculous."

"What gets me most is the way they laugh and brag."

"How can anybody forget the language he's been brought up with?"

"They're traitors, that's all there is to it. Whether they know it or not, they're the advance scouts of the gringos, sent to take our land away from us."

"How the women put up with them is more than I can see" (1963: 135–136).

But Damían takes a different view of his experience in the United States:

"No, Padre, I'm sorry to say so, but when we come back, we realize what the people here have to put up with, the injustice and the living conditions. Why should a man have to sweat all day to earn a few cents? And sometimes not even that. The rich are past masters at juggling accounts, and put the peasants off with promises they don't mean to keep, stop their mouths with enough corn and beans that they won't die of hunger, and just say, 'We'll see . . . at harvest time . . . next year . . .' If they struggle for it they may get a few yards of coarse cotton cloth, and a few more of cheap percale, but their debts are never paid, they're handed on from father to son. You never have a house of your own, and if you do manage to get a little plot of land, you're forced to sell it for less than you paid for it, tricked out of it. The family lives in a hovel, the children grow up there, they have nothing to wear when they're alive and when their time comes, nothing to die in.

"I tell you, Padre, it can't go on like this; sooner or later the worm will turn, and for better or worse, things will change. To be frank, it would be better if the gringos did come and teach us their way of life than for us to stay the way we are now, living no life at all. Who enjoys it? Tell me. The poor? No. Nor the rich either; they don't even know how to spend their money. The women work all the time like slaves, raising families, always wearing black, always afraid to move. What are we working for? The next life? That's all right, but I believe we ought to make this one a little better and live like human beings. Why can't we eat our fill and enjoy it, have a drink now and then, have some fun for a change, sing, visit, speak our minds, talk to women, wear decent clothes that fit us, work in freedom like the gringos? They at least aren't hypocrites. Here life is always sad, we sigh without knowing why, we don't even dare to draw a free breath. We take pleasure in making ourselves suffer.

"This is no life, Padre, forgive me. Those of us who have known what freedom is will never be satisfied with these customs again. No. The worst sin is exploiting others, and the sin is greater when it's hand in hand with hypocrisy. Don't tell me that the men here don't feel like men, or feel their gorge rising, just because, outwardly, they pretend to be meek. Don't even try to tell me that about the women. The saint that slips is soon a devil, as the saying goes, begging your pardon. You can do anything if you go about it the right way, but pretense and the use of force make matters worse; a rope strained too much will break. Many of the women who have run away, so many unhappy women, might have had a happier lot if they'd been allowed to behave according to their feelings and hadn't been forced to pretend.

"We who have been away are criticized because we see how things are and speak out. But this state of affairs can't go on. Oh, I agree that nobody here dies of hunger, but don't tell me that most people are doing more than barely living. You know as well as I do how they struggle and worry for half enough to live on. But go to Cuernavaca, Puebla, Chihua-hua, where I worked, and you'll really see hell let loose, on the sugar farms, the huge estates. The people live worse than slaves. If anyone so much as opens his mouth, he's stabbed to death or beaten till he's half-dead. I saw tortures worse than the Christian martyrs went through. You don't realize what's going on in other parts of the Republic; when the Revolution starts it will catch us unawares here. Mexico isn't just our region, and you priests, begging your pardon, ought not to pull the wool over the people's eyes.

"I won't deny that life can be hard in the United States; but you can live in comfort and freedom. I'm not denying, either, that in some parts of the United States, especially in Texas and California, there are people who think Mexicans are no more than animals; there're a great many Mexicans there and they have our Mexican faults. But if you go a little farther north, you'll see how different it is; besides, even in Texas and California it depends on the place you make for yourself. I could live there comfortably enough. They say that the money we earn there has wings; the truth is, it's in our blood to spend it as fast as we get it and we can't keep our hands on it; the poorest earns four times as much as he earns here—in ready cash too, not in promises. And when you come back, the minute you reach the border you get a different treatment even from your own fellow countrymen, and you feel let down. That's why so many fellows won't work when they get back but only dream of going away again. Call it whatever you like—Socialism, or Liberalism—but that's the truth. The Church doesn't deny human nature, does it, or want a man to spend all his time praying? Well, then . . . ?" (pp. 136–138).

The negative aspects showing U.S. racial prejudice and ill-treatment of Mexican braceros are balanced in Yáñez's novel, then, with a presentation of the reasons a bracero leaves Mexico in the first place: low wages, injustices suffered, and a wretched life in general. He also pictures a more comfortable life with better wages available to the bracero in the United States. For Yáñez, it would appear, moreover, that the braceros accomplished a liberation of the mind and spirit. They were the transporters of new ideas.

They had begun to think for themselves instead of accepting tradition-ridden and antiquated modes of life.

1913

In the short story "El repatriado" (1960), Rafael F. Múnoz presents a young man of twenty, Andrés, crossing the United States–Mexican border at Juárez, Mexico, after a five-year stay in California. He returns to Mexico eagerly looking forward to seeing his country and his native city, Chihuahua. The year is 1913. On entering Mexico, Andrés finds the country in complete chaos, with civil war underway after the arrest and murder of Francisco I. Madero by General Huerta. There are no trains to take him to his beloved hometown. Instead, he finds soldiers, guns, ammunition, and war activity everywhere. Bewildered at what he encounters, he manages to obtain passage to Chihuahua in a train filled with Huerta's Federal soldiers. Before reaching his city, a battle ensues between Federal soldiers and the rebel contingent led by Pancho Villa. Pancho Villa and his men are victorious and Andrés joins the rebels.

As the rebel troups travel through the hot Chihuahua desert, and as different battles take place along the way, Andrés's desire to see his native city becomes increasingly urgent. Finally, when the rebels reach the outskirts of Chihuahua, Andrés runs to the top of a hill overlooking the city, despite warnings from the soldiers not to do so. His desire to see his city once again becomes the all-encompassing reality for him. After repeated orders from the revolutionary soldiers to come down and Andrés's blatant disregard of these warnings, the order to shoot him is given. Andrés dies on the top of the hill overlooking the city with a serene smile on his face. He is the first of many braceros to die·a violent death in Mexico in the literary works.

The picture here is of a homesick bracero happily looking forward to home and finding instead a war-torn country. Although the story primarily deals with the trip from the United States–Mexican border to the Chihuahua city, and does not describe in detail the experiences of this particular bracero, in the beginning it does describe Andrés as he leaves the United States. The bracero's appearance is caricatured, and his ''Americanized'' aspect is seen in a ridiculous light:

Andrés definitely had the face of a returning Mexican. Underneath a small hat whose brim was ridiculously narrow, one could discern the thick boar-like, black hair. It had been cut in a Buster Brown style and looked like a wig (*peluca*). The false, overstarched collar stood stiffly at his sides as if it were an alabaster base for his dark-skinned face. His blue suit fitted him loosely, like a pillowcase. His shoes were rounded at the tips and his suitcase, bursting at the seams, was tightly bound with wide straps of leather. The Mexican that has worked in the United States and returns (1960:162–163).

The description reflects an animosity and disdain for those who cross the border and return with new cultural acquisitions. The adjectives and adverbs used in this description denote the negative feelings of the author—the suffix "illo" in *sombrerillo* (small hat), for example, having a deprecatory effect. The hat's brim is "ridicula-mente corta" (ridiculously narrow); his hair is like "cerda" (boar's bristles), a "peluca" (wig, a connotation of falseness, arti-ficiality); he wears "un cuello postizo" "rígido por el almidón" (a false, overstarched collar); his suit was "amplio como funda de sillón" (like a pillowcase, loose, ill-fitting). The author wishes to portray his bracero in a most undignified, unkind, and cutting manner.

1933

One of the most vindictive accounts of bracero life came in 1933 with the publishing of Juan Bustillo Oro's drama, "Los que vuel-ven." The first act takes place in the United States in the early 1930s on a huge wheat farm owned by an industrial firm during the period of the Depression. On this farm, Mexican workers are gathering the wheat crop. Among them is a man, Chema, and his wife, Remedios. A rumor is heard that the Mexican workers are going to be deported in order to make room for the jobless United States citizens. At the same time a second rumor is spread that the wheat crop is going to be burned owing to the low price of wheat in the market. At the end of the first act both rumors prove to be true. Repeated references are made to the injustices committed against the Mexican workers and the folly of going to work in a strange and foreign land.

In the second act, Chema and Remedios find themselves in the home of their daughter who has married a North American. They are made to feel extremely unwelcome by their son-in-law and finally he calls the immigration officers in order to have them deported. Chema and Remedios refuse to leave without first finding out about their long-lost son, but it is all to no avail. They are deported.

In the third act, Chema finds himself across the border in a Mexican desert. Having lost his wife (Remedios dies on the return trip to Mexico) and his daughter (she stays with her North American husband), and still searching for his lost son, Chema has gradually become mentally unbalanced. In a fit of anger and desperation he grabs a knife and threatens a Mexican guard but is himself shot to death as the play ends. Chema is the second in a series of violent bracero deaths that take place in Mexican territory, Andrés in "El repatriado" being the first one.

Bustillo Oro thus presents the bracero experience in a completely negative manner. For example, we find Chema, the main character, always lamenting the fact that he has left Mexico:

CHEMA: His father committed the same mistake I did, boss. The same . . . that for which the old lady cries . . . throwing our sons into a strange country even though ours is hungering for its own (1933:20).

and again, another character, Garcia, comments:

GARCIA: I tell you, it sure does not feel like we have left Mexico. . . . With you, I feel like I am still there, that I have not come to suffer with the *gringos* (p. 22).

Chema's wife, Remedios, seconds him in regard to this sentiment:

REMEDIOS: At times, this land does not seem to belong to God, and us foreigners, more than anyone else, suffer the consequences (p. 29).

Their son, who has lost a hand while working with machinery, writes them a letter expressing similar sentiments:

PEDRO: These cities are damned because of the insatiable thirst for money ever present. . . . Hunger, Dad, hunger everywhere. . . . That is where their dark ambition took them. . . . And it is those like us that pay for it. . . . The only thing they remember, now that they can no longer use us, is to give us a cup of dirty water and a morsel of bread. This is the "food" we get after spending hours in line among all the other hungry people (p. 31).

It is ironic that both Chema and his son die on the Mexican side of the border while waiting to be transported to their hometowns. The author, having strong Marxist inclinations, presents a caustic indictment against the policies of capitalism in both Mexico and the United States.

Late 1940s

Luis Spota's *Murieron a la mitad del río* (1948) exemplifies novels dealing with the great influx of Mexican labor pouring into the United States after World War II. Such books dealt with the many stories of exploitation, murder, and robbery of braceros in the United States and were scathing indictments of this "traffic in manpower."

Murieron a la mitad del río tells of three young men, José Pavan, Luis Alvarez, and "Cocula," who decide to try to make good in the United States. In crossing the Río Grande River (the river that serves as a natural boundary between the United States and Mexico), Cocula, a homosexual, fails in the first try but stubbornly keeps trying until he makes it. The other two succeed on their first attempt but find in the United States only prejudice, exploitation, and hard times. Traveling from town to town, they experience everywhere humiliation, hunger, and exhausting, interminable work with little or no remuneration. Finally, they decide to go back to Mexico, where a Mexican border policeman robs them, and the Mexican people in the towns scorn them. Deciding to try their luck again in the United States, they attempt to swim across the river. Luis is shot and killed by a border patrolman just after reaching the American side. Pavan decides to go it alone but, after roaming the countryside without any luck, he returns to Mexico. Bitter and sad, he vows never to return.

In Héctor Raúl Almanza's novel about the late 1940s, *Huelga blanca* (1950), we have a work depicting the experiences of Felipe García and Martín Guerrero in the Rio Grande Valley of Texas. Although the book does not deal in its entirety with the bracero experience, it does describe the lives of the two main characters while briefly in the United States.

Felipe and Martín have left Parangaricutiro, Michoacán, to go to the northern part of Mexico to seek their fortunes. They stop to work for a time on the fertile farms of the state of Tamaulipas near the United States–Mexican border. After the harvest they decide to go to the United States, the "fabulous country" across the river of which they have heard so much from their fellow countrymen. One of the young men, Felipe, has a special interest in going to work in the United States because he seeks to marry Sabina, the daughter of the farmer for whom he worked in Tamaulipas.

The two cross the river eagerly looking forward to earning plenty of dollars. As luck would have it, though, the young men, unfamiliar with the terrain, are soon lost in a citrus grove. Here, they encounter their first bout with prejudice on meeting a man of Mexican extraction. Felipe and Martín, expecting him to be friendly since they recognize their common ethnic background, ask him for directions and about the possibility of finding work. The Mexican-American, however, shows no sign of recognition and instead mistreats them verbally and threatens to shoot them if they do not leave the grove immediately. Both young men are first bewildered, then hurt, and finally angered at the man who, although ethnically resembling them, shows no sign of friendliness; on the contrary, he seems brutal and inhuman. They leave the grove shocked but a little less naïve about what to expect in the United States.

After many hardships, Felipe and Martín manage to secure employment in an ill-paying job:

For a few days they harvested potatoes. Under the heavy metallic rays of the sun, they spent the whole day stooped to the ground, pulling the heavy potato-laden sacks, all this so they could earn twenty-five cents. This was but half the minimum wage that was customarily paid to American workers (1950:27–28).

In Almanza's view:

Wetbacks like Felipe and Martín, whose relations with the local author-ities can never be altogether friendly, are doomed to execute the most difficult and humble work, at the lowest possible wages. The employers become aware of their illegal status and do not hesitate to take advantage of them (p. 28).

This period of employment does not last long, however, and soon both are deported without earning the desired amount of money. Not having enough for the fare home to Parangaricutiro, Michoa-cán, Felipe and Martín decide to seek employment on the same farm where they had worked before departing for the United States. The farmer, Severo Martínez, realizing the possibility of the advantages of having two strong hands around to help with his cotton lands, offers them a partnership in his farm. The partner-ship consists of the boys working at clearing the land, planting it, and, at the end of the year, dividing the profits.

When picking time comes, however, a problem arises over the cotton prices. The Mexican government sets the price to be paid for cotton. The gin owners do not want to pay this price and refuse to buy the cotton brought in by the farmers. The same gin owners lead the peasants to believe that it is the government who is inter-fering with the buying and selling of cotton, goading them into a strike against the Mexican government. Felipe becomes aware of this deceit and decides to inform the rest of the farmers, but he is knifed to death by one of the hoodlums hired by the unfeeling, greedy gin owners. With Felipe out of the way the government gives in to the strike and revokes its decree calling for high prices to be paid to the peasants for their cotton crop. The bracero experience in the United States and the farming experience in Mexico are presented in completely gloomy terms. There is no humor, no kindness, no sense of shared humanity anywhere, the bracero experience being painful on both sides of the border.

Jesús Topete's *Aventuras de un bracero* (1949) differs from the other works in one important respect. It is written as if by a bracero who has decided to write a personal account of his experiences in the United States. The novel is, therefore, written in a breezy, humorous style, trying, as best as possible, to imitate the speech of a bracero. But the bracero depicted is atypical for most braceros did not have the educational training displayed by Topete's bracero. Topete's 143-page work, nevertheless, yields a fine summary of many unhappy experiences of a bracero. It merits detailed analysis.

There is an introduction by Gutierre Tibón which strikes an ironic note, considering what is to follow. Tibón describes the bracero in positive terms, noting that he is "made of excellent human fiber, blessed with a noble interior life, and sensibility and courage that in a near future, once polished, will astonish the world." The book itself is divided into eleven chapters, each depicting the most salient aspects of the "bracero experience" from his obtaining a contract in Mexico, to his working sojourn in California, to his return trip to Mexico. Chapter one aims criticism at the Mexican government and its corrupt officials who do not hesitate to extract the last penny from the poverty-stricken braceros in return for a contract. There is even a sad commentary on the frailties of human nature as a whole. The bracero himself is humorously criticized, for example, for being such a fool for going to the United States "where the hook with the dangling dollar was taking thousands upon thousands of Mexicans" (1948:5).

The sufferings and travails of the waiting braceros are duly noted:

The crowd [of braceros], a sweaty and hungry, was always standing in lines, sometimes four deep, lines which had formed around the stadium and which were hundreds of meters long. Some were there for as long as eight days standing in line, hours and hours. They would spend the night there in place where all the bodily functions were carried out on the spot. There the taco sellers would travel back and forth servicing all the lines of men which the police gamely tried to keep in order with their guns and tear gas (pp. 6–7).

The fleecing of the braceros by their own countrymen is likewise criticized.

Here and there one could see groups of men that were around someone wearing a ragged jacket who, with a studied mysterious tone, would murmur a word of promise and then quickly pocket a few dirty and sweaty pesos extracted from some poor victim. The happy victims would smile upon hearing the false words of assurance, dreaming of having a contract in their hands and going to California (pp. 7–8).

The bracero is criticized for being a rogue. A sad scene at trainside in a Mexican railroad stop is described in the following passage:

Something I will never forget, and which to tell the truth truly made me feel some sort of shame to be part of this caravan, is the scene that would take place when the train stopped at a station and some women selling tacos or other things would approach it. Also there were poverty-stricken families that would wait for the trains to see if they could see their father, brother, son, or boyfriend who had abandoned them to go in search of the dollar with which they hoped to solve their problems. I was saying . . . that truly when we are gathered in large groups, the impunity that numbers provide converts us into vandals. It was not just obscenities that those who were near the train had to bear, but many times some taco-selling women would get too close to the train cars in order to sell more and that is when . . . [the braceros] would paw them, get fresh with them, and the women would come from the crowd of men crying without tacos or money and with dresses torn (pp. 13–14).

Aside from being a scathing indictment of human nature the scene serves as a general criticism of the bracero experience, which in the author's opinion, reduced humanity to its lowest level. The general desolation and sufferings of the women trying to catch a final glimpse of a beloved male as he left for the United States further emphasizes the negative aspects of the experience. The spectacle produces in the reader a sense of sadness and pity. An important result of the departure scene is to provide a glimpse of a bracero with human failings and less a spiritless, faceless entity shown in some of the other works.

Chapter Two underlines the humiliation suffered by the braceros as they arrive in Nogales and travel to California. Three significant passages point this out. In the first instance, female U.S. border inspectors are repelled by the braceros: "A few tall, serious, blond women dressed in uniform and carrying guns, sporting rubber gloves and a grimace of disgust or revulsion, searched our suitcases, packages, or bags, and anything that was part of our luggage" (p. 17). In the second instance, the braceros' humiliation results from criticism of their *machismo*, their super masculine ego. Braceros were forewarned not to flirt or talk with the young women on the streets while traveling: "Whoever pesters the women around the stations will be taken off the train, thrown into jail, and thereafter taken back to Mexico.'' And when some did not heed the warning:

We soon found out that the gringo meant what he said. In one of the cars up front, some men took the liberty in one of the stations to say something to some blond women. The women in turn complained to the conductor. The train stopped. The police came in and those braceros that were pointed out by the women as being the culprits were forced to step down. And only two men that got on their knees and asked forgiveness were allowed to continue. The others were taken by the police (p. 18).

The third humiliation the braceros suffer comes when they are mocked and openly ridiculed:

Frequently, some people would look out their windows to see our troop. Others would stop on the sidewalks laughing at us and pointing at those men without shoes. They would burst out laughing having a good time at our expense. This was not a pretty picture, one can say, but since we had no choice there was nothing left to do but look the other way and put up with it (p. 21).

This novelistic experience is comparable to an actual experience given in my composite picture of a bracero in the next chapter.

In the third chapter, Topete describes the arrival of the braceros in the Mandeville Islands[?] where they were assigned to work. The housing available to the workers is nothing to brag about. In Topete's words:

Upon seeing the house in which we were to take residence that night and all the others to come, my hair stood on end because the place looked more like a pigsty or a witch's house than anything else. There were no window panes, the door creaked, and there were holes and cobwebs everywhere, even in our cots. Even though we were dead tired from all the days and nights we had been traveling, when we saw those cots we suddenly did not feel tired. But that was nothing; what really killed our desire to lie down was the bitter cold that had made our feet and jaws frozen stiff (p. 23).

Of particular interest in Chapter Three is the description of the foreman of the company, Mister Tikler, the only American who comes in direct working contact with the braceros. He is described in the most generous terms, in sharp contrast with the accounts given of a Filipino foreman and of the pochos or Chicanos in general.

[Mr. Tikler is] a man about half a century old—a kindly man of intelligent demeanor and a hard worker who inspired sympathy in all of us to such an extent that because of his kindly treatment many stayed in that place in spite of the Filipino who was . . . a mule.

Mister Tikler is a technician when it comes to agriculture. He knows so much about the mechanical workings of machines that I thought there was not one machine that Mr. Tikler did not know. On many occasions I saw him myself when he was fixing a tractor, afterward a truck, and someone told me he designed agricultural machines. He always carried out his tasks with cleanliness and speed. He could use the acetylene torch, solder electrical wirings including automobile wiring and did riveting whenever it became necessary.

His kindly demeanor was immediately in his favor and, as I said earlier, the way he treated us was the primary factor that induced us to stay working in that camp.

According to him he came from a German family, and during peace time he worked for the government. He owns a farm, which he runs with the help of his relatives and works there in addition to his other jobs.

My conversations with Mr. Tikler were one of the reasons for my study of English. I was hoping to understand more of what he said. In the beginning I was constantly answering "yes" to everything he said (pp. 32–33).

Chapter Four is a short chapter (pp. 34–39) depicting the hardships of the braceros trying to adjust to the freezing temperatures typical of the Mandeville Islands in wintertime. Owing to the inclement weather, the braceros mostly waited around in their shacks trying to kill time by playing cards, singing, and so on. Eventually, as winter turns to spring and spring to summer, the braceros find themselves picking potatoes under the hot rays of the sun.

Much of Chapter Five is devoted to Chicanos. Topete introduces the section on pochos by stating that the braceros were told some young ladies were coming to work with them. Topete expects to see some Anglo girls like those appearing in the movies, so beautiful that they keep one awake at night. But the braceros were completely disappointed:

When I saw those bodies that looked like tadpoles with Chichimec faces speaking English in loud voices, and wearing pants and boots, I could not tell whether they were men or women. What they had of femininity one could not see. In truth many of the braceros were prettier than they were.

It would be unfair to say all were like that; there were some exceptions. Some were passable enough to look at without wincing.

They arrived speaking English and, at anything the men asked them, they would shrug their shoulders saying they did not understand. Some of them, when in front of gringos, they would start talking "in Spanish." Probably in order to brag. Because the type of people that we generally know as pochos are made up one hundred percent of vain bragging and fatuity. Some braceros started to befriend the pochas even though I assured them that they thought we were a bunch of poverty-stricken men that had just come down from the hills.

I have lived in Guadalajara most of my life. It is a large city famous for its pretty women. Thus those fat women of most undesirable personality did not attract me (pp. 48–49).

Topete is particularly annoyed at the way Chicanos speak: "Naturally, when they were talking, they would mix their English with their Spanish, pretending they were Yankees" (pp. 49–50). Chicanas were chastised for their supposed "ugliness" and their inability to speak "correct" Spanish. In addition Topete describes in detail the personality of a Mexican who has become a pocho by virtue of having lived in the United States for forty years:

With respect to that type of creature [Chicano] I had a few facts. There were two of them in the camp when we arrived. There was one that had been living in the United States for more than forty years and who had become a naturalized citizen. He did not have any family. He used to talk about the horrors of Mexico and the Mexicans whom he characterized as a bunch of poverty-stricken, dirty people. The other one was a real pocho, born in the United States of Mexican parents. He was scheming, hypocritical, glib, and a cheat who picked clean many of my friends. He would ask some of the braceros to go out to drink so that they would pay for his drinks. Finally they caught him stealing from one of our bracero countrymen whom he had gotten drunk. The police took him away.

I insist on speaking about pochos because I studied them in detail and no matter which side I observed I could not find anything but the most despicable characteristics.

One day I let out all that I felt about such beings when one of the girls came to ask me who did I think I was that I did not talk to them. She wanted to know why I acted so proud and did not deign to visit with them. To which I more or less answered:

—I do not like anybody poking fun at me. I do not believe there is anything funny about me. You have enough men to laugh about. On the other hand I do not like to talk to you because all you do is brag and humiliate us. In front of gringos you pretend to be Mexican and maybe amongst yourselves you believe this to be so, but when you meet Mexicans you start talking in English pretending you are gringas. You do not know how to speak English because although I do not know much, I can tell. You do not know how to speak Spanish because what you say in Spanish is a mixture of Caló[2] found amongst the criminal element and the terminology used is that of the most remote parts of Mexico in the ranches and mountains of Mexico. I am not awed by you, and do not

[2]Caló is a form of slang spoken in the different barrios of the Spanish-speaking world.

take you for gringas as you might think I do, because that Totonaca-like Indian face one can tell three kilometers away (pp. 50–52).

In spite of the antagonism between braceros and Chicanas described in Topete's book and others it is commonly acknowledged that many braceros married Chicanas and thus established permanent homes in the United States. But, thoroughly disgusted with Chicanos, Topete ends the chapter by praising Mexico and wishing Chicanos would leave Mexico alone and never mention the fact that they are of Mexican descent. "That disgust they hold for Mexico, so unjustified as well as stupid, is what makes that race so hateful" (p. 52).

Topete's sixth chapter dwells on the topic of food. Since the braceros described in the novel work for a company rather than for an individual farmer, the braceros eat at a cafeteria-style dining area in a kitchen manned by cooks. In Topete's novel, the food is atrocious in addition to being skimpy. The Filipino foreman and his wife, who were in charge of feeding the braceros, would siphon off the groceries destined to feed the braceros and sell a major portion to local stores.

Chapters Seven and Eight deal with the more or less happy adventures of the bracero-narrator. Topete and his friends take a trip to Stockton and San Francisco where they try to have as much fun as possible.

Chapter Nine details the excessively hard work expected of braceros and describes the arduous task of potato-picking:

In order to pick potatoes you tie a belt around your waist. The belt has a board in front with two hooks on either side and on the ground is a whole bunch of empty gunnysacks. The gunnysacks are placed on the hooks on the board. To pick, you bend down and crawl, scratching the earth with your fingernails, moving your hands rapidly. The potatoes are thrown inside the bag and when it's almost full it is put aside and an empty bag takes its place. This is done all day, the hot sun striking the bowed back seemingly melting your whole body. Both face and body are covered with a thick layer of mud which forms from the mixture of sweat and dirt. The mud irritates your face due to the fertilizers in it which produce a burning sensation like hot pepper or raw lime.

Writing this is easy, but when you are kneeling for hours, and scratching the earth like dogs, your kidneys feel like burning coals. And when you get up to change sacks, you feel dizzy enough to fall to the ground. However, right behind come the trucks that pick up the potato sacks. Up front the caterpillar moves the earth to expose the potatoes, the foreman yelling at the workers not to waste time. You may feel like dying of heat and thirst, and from exhaustion, but if you can still move you have to continue working.

I always considered that work the heaviest, and my hunch was confirmed when many of the boys fainted in the fields. Some fainted after working only half a day. I said I considered this work to be the heaviest but in reality I was mistaken. There was another job that was bad enough for anyone to ask for immediate medical or even spiritual help.

I am referring to the task of picking up the filled potato sacks and throwing them into the trucks. That really finishes you off. With those two jobs I became convinced that the illustrious Torquemada, inventor of the Inquisition and expert in inserting live coals in the intestines of heretics, putting out the eyes with hot iron rods, and other such activities, had fallen far short in his inventions. If he had returned from the grave to take a look at the potato pickers he would have been touched and would have exclaimed, "What infamy!" as he dropped dead from the sight (pp. 112–114).

Chapter Ten covers a successful strike organized by braceros against low pay and the harsh nature of the work. Topete's most caustic criticism in this chapter is directed toward the Mexican inspectors, who sided with the company and not with the braceros:

The Farm Work Inspectors were like a plague. They were a bunch of bribe-takers worse than the Filipinos and treated the braceros, I think, as if they were inmates from the prison of the Islas Marías. At least the ones that were in that area. They were a despotic bunch whom you couldn't even talk to let alone contradict or explain anything to. They sided with the gringo bosses even more than did the Yankees or the Filipinos (pp. 123–124).

As soon as these *inspectores* arrived, they started telling us that that was not the way to pay back the hospitality afforded us; that the food was great and cheap; that the lodgings were clean and well furnished; that the work wasn't that hard and was well paid; that they were surprised how men who were accustomed to eating only beans in Mexico and who slept on the floor on a straw mat could complain about the food and board which was far beyond any of their expectations; and in addition to all this, earning so much money, which we had never even dreamed of earning in such magnificent circumstances (pp. 123–124).

The final chapter brings the bracero back to where he started in Mexico. Topete again describes the corruption exhibited by the Mexican officials who are eager to extract what they can from the bracero:

We were lined up in order to have our luggage inspected. I had been afraid of this because I had been told of the many things that were taken away [from the returned braceros]. But actually . . . [the customs officials] weren't that strict. In a low voice the customs officials would tell us to give them a bribe and they would not inspect us. And that did it! those bribes convinced me that my joy was not in vain, that I was not dreaming, that I was finally back in Mexico (p. 139).

Although Topete depicts the braceros plight, his heavy emphasis on the negative turns his work into another not very well-written novel of social protest. The braceros depicted lack the universal human characteristics that can help them transcend Topete's novel. They are types instead of rounded human beings.

Early 1950s

In a 1958 novel by Carlos Fuentes, translated in 1960 as *Where the Air Is Clear,* the action takes place in 1951. The bracero is presented as a representative of a Mexican social class, with Fuentes presenting the different classes found in present-day Mexico and showing the failure of the Revolution and of its leaders to eradicate the sharp and unjust differences in classes and to provide the peasant the opportunity for a better life, as promised. The bracero in this novel represents one of the many unfortunate Mexicans belonging to the lower class. He represents a class that knows only drabness, extreme poverty, illness, and the ever present hand of death.

Still, Fuentes describes both the negative and positive aspects of the bracero experience. His bracero, Gabriel, returns bitter from his encounter with prejudice but is aware, nevertheless, of the advantages found in the United States, and he realizes that prejudice is rampant in Mexico too. Gabriel states: "And he had said to Tuno, when they were together at harvest time in Texas, 'So what if they don't let you in their crappy restaurants? You able to get in the Ambassador in Mexico City?'" (1960:31). Gabriel, a recent arrival from the United States, is presented as a typical bracero happy upon his return to his native country and eager to show off the acquisitions he has brought with him. They consist of both material goods such as radios, electrical appliances, clothing, and his ability to speak a few phrases in English. In attempting to show how the electrical appliances work and finding no electricity, Gabriel expresses the sentiment of many a bracero: "He would not change Mexican cooking for anything, but next year once again he would take off northward, to the land where there was work and money, and electricity" (p. 32).

Fuentes, thus, presents the different sides of the bracero story: the bitter, hurt side exposed to prejudice and ill-treatment, and the happy satisfied side of the bracero who has been able to work and has been able to accumulate tangible material goods as a result of his labor. Too, he gives the reasons for the bracero exodus to a strange and foreign country. For Fuentes's Gabriel, immigration involved a wad of dollars in his pocket and shining presents so he and his family could all live better. "It was his first year, and he had brought back everything he could carry legal or contraband, risking bullets and drowning when he crossed the Rio. Well, it was that or push an ice-cream cart along the streets of Mexico City" (p. 31). Gabriel's desire to return to the United States was not to be granted for he was knifed to death in a senseless barroom brawl. Gabriel is another of the fictional braceros who die a violent death in Mexico.

Juan Rulfo's short story, "Paso del Norte" (1967), deals with an anonymous young man who wants to go to the United States in the early 1950s. We are introduced to him at the point where he is making his wishes known to his father. His father advises him against going, but the young bracero decides to make the trip in spite of parental advice. He departs for the United States, leaving his wife and children in his father's care. The adventurous young man joins another bracero and together they decide to cross the Río Grande River. As they are attempting to cross the river, they are shot, the bracero is killed and the young man is wounded. The principal character manages to escape and returns to tell his father of the mishap. His father informs him that his wife has run away with another man whereupon the son matter-of-factly decides to go look for her.

This short story is an excellent example of Juan Rulfo's work. He presents both sides of the bracero experience. On the positive side we are informed humorously by Rulfo's character that in the United States money is available if one works. The father asks: "And what the devil are you going to do up North?" He answers: "Well, make money. You know Carmelo came back rich, even brought back a phonograph, and he charges five centavos to listen to the music. Five centavos for every number, from a Cuban dance to that Anderson woman who sings sad songs—the same for all of them—and he makes good money and they even line up to listen. So you see, you just have to go and come back. That's why I'm going" (p. 148). On the negative side we have the tragedy of a nameless bracero who loses his life while attempting to enter the United States. In addition, the separation of families with its tragic consequences is also presented.

A 1956 novel *Tenemos sed* by Magdalena Mondragón is very one-sided in its view of the bracero experience, even though Mondragón won the prize granted in 1954 by the Mexican newspaper *El Nacional* for writing it. The novel deals primarily with the state of Tamaulipas, the destruction of Ciudad Guerrero by the flowing waters of the Río Grande river, the construction of Falcon Dam, and the construction of a new city.

In one chapter Mondragón deals with a bracero, Teófilo Aguirre, who together with his wife and child, crosses the river. Teófilo is described by the author as a greedy grasping man who had no reason whatsoever for leaving his native country. According to Mondragón, "Teófilo Aguirre was a specialized driller. He could and always had earned good wages. But he wanted more. He dreamt of coming back home to his loved ones loaded with dollars after having worked his heart out in a meagerly paying job. He would have sold his soul to the devil in exchange for instant riches" (p. 124).

Teófilo manages to cross the river together with his wife and child but is immediately caught by the border patrol and detained in a concentration camp. The conditions in which they are held are described as atrocious. Teófilo's baby dies of pneumonia without the benefit of medical help. After the painful stay in this concentration camp, the parents are deported to Ciudad Guerrero where they begin life anew, seeking employment and a place to live.

As can be seen, this is one of the novels presenting the bracero experience in totally black terms. While Teófilo is crossing the river we are given the following description:

Before this, he had thought perhaps people exaggerated. But now he knew the stories told fell short of the truth. No one could describe that fear felt toward the unknown. It was not like fighting face to face with a man . . . with a hundred men. It was the bullet hitting its mark in the darkness. It was one's own countrymen disguised as bandits waiting, searching for men along the river, to see who had arrived with sufficient dollars to make his murder worthwhile; and afterward discarding the body in the river to be swallowed in the darkness and lost forever. It was the sharp blade and the inhuman trickery.

Afterward . . . the unscrupulous contracting, the complaints lodged and left unanswered, the anguish, the indifference, and always or almost always, death. . . . (p. 125).

In another passage Mondragón writes:

They were pushed, kicked, and insulted inside the camp. Keeping the bracero out was an expensive business. Perhaps they were right in insulting them. They deserved that and much more for being such fools.

And in there he learned many things. The final results of that tragic journey. Those that died while crossing the border, murdered by the border patrol; those that died at the hands of their own countrymen; those that were recruited into concentration camps due to their illegal status; those that were contracted illegally and exploited as modern age slaves without any rights whatsoever. Those that were sent to Alaska . . . those that were no more. . . . Men, good men, magnificent men at the edge of the law, marked, wounded, humiliated. Damned, exiled one! It is their own making. . . . With no rights whatsoever! (p. 133).

In "Brazos que se van" and "Pobre patria mía," María Luisa Melo de Remes shows a more balanced approach. Plausible reasons are cited for a bracero leaving in the first place. In "Brazos que se van" (1955a) the story takes the form of a dialogue between Melo de Remes and a bracero she has hired to clear her yard and tend her trees. The bracero informs her that he is working temporarily in Mexico because his desire is to go back to the United States. She proceeds to recount the negative aspects of the bracero experience in the United States: prejudice, ill-treatment, hard work. The bracero answers with his reasons for leaving: inability to obtain work and low wages in Mexico compared with availability of a steady job and reasonable pay in the United States. The dialogue takes the following form:

When I pointed out that migrating was a difficult undertaking, that many atrocious acts were committed against our farm workers, he responded with a sigh and with painful indignation:

"More difficult than life here in Mexico? Do not believe it. There, in the United States, we can at least drink milk and eat ham. Besides, there is not a single Mexican that goes to work for the gringo that does not return with a new jacket. . . ." He continued as if he had read my thoughts on the recent discriminatory acts committed against our braceros in Texas, acts that the government has started to investigate:

"Let's not fool ourselves. No matter how hard the farmworker tries here, he cannot prosper. If it does not rain, the crop dies; if it rains and the crop is harvested, well then, the profit is spent on repaying the 'Bank' and we end up owing them to boot! That is why, ten years ago, I decided to go pick lettuce in the Imperial Valley. I was very happy to work and I earned a lot of money then! But as all good things must come to an end, one day the long arm of the immigration officers caught me and I landed feet first in Algodones, México" (pp. 14–15).

The author concludes that although it is a painful fact to admit, the bracero's reasoning and observations are correct and justified. She concludes with a note of sad resignation:

And I will have to live with my pain, because those trees will undoubtly die. My neighbor will not find a gardener as competent as Chuy, because all those excellent working arms will leave. Today they not only escape to our northern neighbor in search of better salaries, but long to live amongst the green foliage of corn that belongs to another. They carry with them a deep resentment against their country. The injustices and harassment received in their own country have made them bitter against their land (p. 19).

In "Pobre patria mía" (1955*b*), Melo de Remes also presents both sides of the bracero experience. The story is written in anecdote form. The author relates a painful experience she had while crossing the United States–Mexican border at San Ysidro, California, on her way to visit friends on the American side. She tells of her feelings on seeing a group of wretched-looking Mexican nationals being pushed, shoved, and insulted. She wonders why the men leave Mexico in the first place. She finds the answer when she visits the prosperous fertile farm of a Mexican-American. Here the Mexican-American explains the opportunities provided by the United States to farmers which enable them to prosper while contrasting a neighboring barren Mexican farm. The Mexican-American farmer states: "The same earth! The same race! Except that there in Mexico, there are no guarantees protecting the farmer; guarantees that would prevent the need for his desperate escape into a foreign land" (p. 78).

In *El dólar viene del norte* (1954), J. de Jesús Becerra González, presents episode after episode depicting negative aspects of bracero experiences. Agustín Carranza, the principal character, returns to his village in Jalisco after he met with an accident while in the United States. On seeing familiar surroundings, he starts to recall all his past life with emphasis on the events that took him to the United States and the experiences he suffered there. Agustín recalls that an unusually prolonged Mexican dry spell resulting in a poor harvest caused his family to fall deeper and deeper in debt and gradually to lose all they had. Finally, an epidemic of *fiebre aftosa* (hoof and mouth disease which affects only cloven-hoofed animals such as cows, pigs, goats, and sheep) took away their last source of livelihood and Agustín was forced to seek employment outside Mexico since throughout the entire area around his native state of Jalisco similar conditions prevailed.

Hearing about the United States from returned braceros, Agustín learned of the "easy money" that could be obtained, and decided to make the trip. He found work in Colton, California, where he was able to stay for three months before being deported. He returned to the United States via Phoenix, Arizona, but again was deported after a short stay. His next try was at Brawley, California. Each time Agustín crossed the border he was caught and deported by U.S. immigration officials, usually without having made any money in the United States. Undaunted by this rash of hard luck, Agustín decided to try again and to head for Los Angeles, hoping that in that sprawling city, with its large Latin population, the immigration officers would not be able to spot him as easily as in the fields. Unfortunately, he was arrested before reaching his destination. Caught at Pendleton Beach, Agustín was suspected of being a spy and was jailed. After being cleared of the spy charges, he was handed over to local immigration officers who jailed him on charges of breaking immigration laws.

In jail Agustín met five other prisoners who had experienced similar difficulties and suffering in the United States, each bracero relating his life history and how he happened to find himself in jail. These individuals came from four different states to depict different types of histories and personalities. The four states—Jalisco, Guanajuato, Michoacán, and Zacatecas—were the states that sent the most braceros to the United States.

After his detention, Agustín was deported, and then for the fifth time he again decided to return to the United States, but he falls off a U.S. train and loses his memory. A Mexican-American doctor took care of Agustín until he decided to leave for Mexico in search of his identity.

In Mexico Agustín, the narrative now having caught up with the opening of the book, is spotted by a cousin who informs him of his identity and his family. He returns home to Jalisco to learn that his wife and son are dead. Not caring what happens to him anymore, he returns to the United States–Mexican border arriving at Nuevo Laredo, México. Here, accompanied by another fellow bracero, he attempts to cross the river. Agustín's companion becomes encircled in a whirlpool as they are crossing the river. As Agustín attempts to save his companion he gets caught in the deep swirling waters and both men drown.

In sum, for Becerra González there is not a single happy note in the whole bracero experience. The bracero presented is kicked from one place to another until he tragically dies while attempting to cross the river to the United States. The sixth crossing proves fatal.

The Bracero Image

Of the intellectual elites examined here, Juan Rulfo, Carlos Fuentes, and Agustín Yáñez seem to know the psycholgical workings of the bracero compared with the rest of the authors who show only a caricature of a bracero. Juan Rulfo depicts the bracero as a peasant with the flavor of the country evident in his language, his humor, and his stoicism. Agustín Yáñez shows a small-town bracero more urbanized and aware of political ideas, and Carlos Fuentes portrays a sophisticated, cynical bracero.

The main themes found in all of the bracero fiction, however, deal with prejudice, ill-treatment, and poor wages, and in general present the bracero experience as a wretched and unbearable one. The theme of prejudice against braceros is exhibited by gringos and by pochos. Almanza describes prejudice by pochos as follows:

Felipe and Martin look at [the pocho] and are startled by what they see. Their previous adventure had not prepared them to deal with, or to understand, the deep hostility that is within the Texan-Mexican. A hostility they harbor against those that carry the same genetic traits and are of the same nationality and of which [Texan-Mexicans] are ashamed. They were not aware of how those poor expatriots are pained by and outraged at having to carry the telltale marks of a dark skin and mixed blood. The Texan-Mexicans find this situation intolerable. Felipe and Martin could not imagine how the Texan-Mexican, by harassing and despising those that carry the same traits, thought they were vindicating themselves and making themselves worthy of their white masters—masters whom they venerate and hate at the same time. The Texan-Mexicans are victims of racial discrimination which exposes them to the hatred of the Texans of European ancestry. They become contaminated with this ugly prejudice. And hating themselves even more than their master, the Texan-Mexicans harbor an inferiority complex which may not be verbally expressed but which they nevertheless feel. The two men from Michoacán were soon to feel the outward manifestations of this inferiority complex (1950, p. 25).

Luis Spota presents this prejudice when one of his main characters tells his friend about a pocho: "[He is the] same as the gringo: hypocrite. Those are the worst. They lick their patron's boots and kick us around even though they are as Mexican as we are—as Indian as we are. Watch out for him and his gossip" (1948, p. 216).

In sum, Mexican intellectuals tended to portray the bracero as a victim of U.S. prejudice usually coming from Chicanos! In order to protect braceros and to encourage their return to Mexico, in the emerging lore of the Mexican elite those braceros who remained in the United States were often seen as traitors to their culture— pochos living without possibility of redemption. This lore has tended to brand both the bracero experience and the Chicano heritage, then, as something less than worthy.

Part Two

FOLKLORE

2

An Oral History Interview with
a Composite Bracero

Let us test elitelore about the bracero experience by developing a composite lore of bracero life as told in their own words by several braceros.

Procedure

The bracero point of view was compiled from field research during the summer of 1969 in Huecorio, Michoacán, Mexico. Huecorio was chosen for various reasons:

It was located in one of the economically depressed states that had sent a large number of braceros to the United States.
It was a small, peasant mestizo village with a population of 844 persons that could easily be handled by one researcher.
Extensive research into its population composition, economy, and social stratification had been conducted in the 1960s by Professor Michael Belshaw, Department of Economics, Hunter College City University of New York, and published in his book A *Village Economy Land and People of Huecorio* (1967).

Every family in Huecorio without exception was acquainted with the United States either through a close relative who had made the trip or through personal experience. (At the time of my research there were forty-five Huecorio residents working in the United States either legally or illegally.) Therefore, it was easy to find males of all ages who had been to the United States and could relate their experiences. The interviewees were chosen with the idea of obtaining as representative a cross-section of Huecorio residents and braceros in general as possible. The factors influencing the choice of interviewees were the following:

Age: 28–56

Address in Huecorio (attempt was made to interview braceros from the various parts of town)

States in the United States visited

Education

Reason for going to the United States

Epoch in which they were in the United States (1947–1963)

My grandfather, José Pablo Tarango, who himself had been a bracero, accompanied me to the village of Huecorio. I decided to enter the small village in the company of my grandfather for two important reasons: (1) my grandfather's experience and background as a bracero allowed him to have an instant rapport with other braceros. He was able to quickly make my initial contacts with the local citizens. (2) I was afraid that my being a young unmarried female interviewing male braceros might be frowned upon by the villagers, particularly the women. My grandfather's presence provided the respectability I needed in order to gain proper acceptance in the community. This proved to be a very important part of my procedure.

We arrived in the small village and my grandfather contacted the mayor of Huecorio and explained my project and the purpose of my visit to the town. The mayor was extremely cordial and helpful, immediately informing me of where I could acquire suitable lodgings for the whole summer. After settling down, it turned out the family with whom I lodged knew each and every household in the village. It was a prominent and prosperous family in Huecorio as well as one of the most admired and popular, and since it knew who had been a bracero and who had not, I could begin at once to select persons to interview from different parts of town in order to assure a cross-sectional view.

Pursuing leads supplied to me by the family with whom I lived, I contacted braceros in their homes or received them in my place of residence, having arranged to reserve a sitting room where I could conduct my interviews with a minimum of interference. A small portable automatic volume-control tape recorder was used, and interviews lasted from half an hour to two and a half hours, the average lasting about one hour and a half. A small remuneration was offered to each bracero after the session, but most of them had been willing and even pleased to do the interviews and thus refused to accept any money. All the braceros seemed very intelligent and eager to talk as can be seen on reading their experiences. I explained the purpose and aims of the project at the beginning of the interview, encouraging each bracero to speak at his own pace and in his own words.

The table summarizes the vital statistics of each bracero. Their names are omitted to protect privacy. As can be seen there was a wide range of ages at the time of the interviews (28–56 years) and at the time the actual bracero trips took place (14–45 years), thus offering a wide spectrum of age experience. Bracero education seems to have been a constant, with about four years of schooling. And the states visited were restricted to the western half of the United States, in particular, California and Texas. The state that the bracero enjoyed most, however, depended even more on the treatment received from the employer than on wages. The braceros interviewed preferred the one-to-one personal relationship with an employer to the impersonal relationship with huge efficient contracting companies.

After transcribing all the interviews, I selected a range of common experiences to form a composite bracero view. This view is expressed in the words of a fictional character named Pedro who recounts his experiences. Pedro's story includes travel and experiences from the different states and the years in which they took place. Included were happy, fruitful experiences as well as empty, sad ones. In short, I have tried to present as wide a spectrum of bracero experiences as possible. A particular effort was made to probe for overtones of racial or cultural animus. The sentences used were actually spoken; the only liberty taken was that of arrangement and the avoidance of duplication.

Pedro's Story

Well, it was like this, *compadre*.[1] Ever since we were children, you know, it was common knowledge that people went up North [to the United States]. In the year 1947, General J. Francisco Múgica was the one that helped us go. He could see how poor people were here. We did not have any work here. Well, you know how they have so many connections and are acquainted with government agencies. He was the one that recommended Huecorio: he talked to the bosses that come from up North. They came seeking to contract the people through him. Since he had promised to help us, the people of Huecorio took courage to make the trip to the North.

Right away, a representative came to see who was going to take charge of the people. He made a list. That is how it started, with a list. All who wanted to go would go write their names. And then,

[1] Technically *compadre* means godfather. It can be used to mean friend, buddy, pal.

Persons Interviewed for Composite View
of Bracero Life

Bracero	Age at time of first trip	Age at time of interview	Years of primary school	Years in U.S.[a]	States visited
1	14	36	4	1947	Montana
2	17	29	4	1957	Texas
3	18	30	3	1957	Texas
4	18	30	4	1957	Michigan California
5	18	46	4	1951-1963	Texas Arkansas California
6	20	37	4	1952-1956	Texas Arkansas California
7	20	38	3	1951-1963	California Michigan Arkansas
8	21	30	4	1957-1963	Michigan California Arizona
9	21	28	4	1962-1963	California Nebraska Colorado
10	22	38	4	1953-1962	Texas Arkansas California
11	23	38	3	1954	California
12	26	48	4	1947-1952	Montana Texas
13	30	52	4	1947-1952	Montana California
14	30	52	3	1947-1952	Montana Arkansas
15	31	38	3	1954-1955	Texas Arkansas
16	45	56	0	1958	Texas Mississippi

[a]Hyphenated years (as in 1951-1963) signify that the bracero made trips off and on to the United States between those dates. It does not mean the bracero stayed without interruption all those years.

well, they could write their names and everything until a list of a hundred or so was filled. Well, right away, right away, "Go to Uruapan!" They sent us over there. The representative who was in charge of the people on the list went and presented all of us to the men at the immigration office.

"Here is the list," we told him.

"Where are you from?" the official asked us.

"From Huecorio. We are sent by General J. Múgica," we told him.

"All right. You wait here. Tomorrow you get to go," he answered.

We waited there. It was not until the next day, about seven o'clock, that we were able to register. Well, he registered all of them. Some had bad luck because they did not come out healthy. There were many requirements to meet there. First thing was our general health. Second were our hands. We would present ourselves there and someone would say, "Let's see!" The Americano would examine our hands. He would feel the texture of our hands: "No," he said, "you are not a farm worker."

Some of the men, eager to get accepted, would take a shovel, a pick, or an axe so as to make blisters and harden the hands. Those that passed the hand test and were found to have hard hands were told, "You go. Go inside." The medical check-up was next. First, the hands, second it was our health.

Well, we all tried and we all made the hand inspection. But with the doctors, well that was another thing. They did not want men who showed so much as a scar on the body. You see, they said that those that had scars were troublemakers. Anyhow, if one of the men had a scar on his body they would ask, "And this? Why you have this? No, we do not want you. You are a troublemaker."

Yes, yes, it was so. There were many requirements. That is why not all made it. Oh, another thing, one time an Americano was about to give the card to a man, to give the card that would allow him to go . . . ,

"Well, it was not to be so. The unfortunate man coughed right in front of the Americano. He coughed right on his face—you know how some people lack manners—yes, he coughed without putting his hand to cover his mouth. Well, the Americano became angry and said, "Hey you! You no good!" The poor man cried. You see, after going through all the trouble and then not to be able to go because he did not cover his mouth when he coughed was too much.

From there, we went on to Irapuato. We traveled by night and we arrived at about one o'clock in the morning. Yes, we went by train. We were happy, compadre, happy to be going to the United States. And we were sure we were going to work. You know how it is, compadre. When one does not know a country and then has the opportunity to go—well, one is very happy!

Yes, we took off. We arrived at Irapuato at about two o'clock in the morning. Yes, they were ready for us there. The Americanos were camped out ready to receive us. On to the Xrays. Well, we—most of us from Huecorio—came out well. Some did not. Some were sick. Their lungs were not well.

In Irapuato they gave us a small paper sack with our lunch and—up you go! We went to the train. We traveled all morning toward Juárez. We traveled day and night. The days seemed so long! Finally, we arrived about four o'clock in the afternoon. After we got down from the train, we went to the camp where they were ready to take us to the offices. They inspected us again to make sure we were not carrying any weapons—guns or knives. Also, we were not to take any fruit. When I was crossing the bridge, there in Juárez, they again stopped me. To inspect me again. It was there that they [the U.S. immigration officials] threw our fruit out into the river. Then we again boarded the train—this time on the other side.

We took off from Juárez. And I noticed how different the United States is from Mexico. There, where the line separates one side—the United States—and the other side—Mexico. Very different! And only the wire in between. How pretty it is!

Well, we traveled day and night. We were all very happy when we arrived at Libes [Libby] Montana. It was there, yes it was there that the interpreter tells us, "You men from Mexico," he says, "how are you doing there?"

"Well, quite all right, Señor," we answered.

"Are you happy?" he asked.

"Yes, sure!" we answered.

"Well, you will be even more happy to know that over there, in the last car, there are some of your countrywomen waiting for you. They have come to greet you!" he told us.

"Well," all of us started yelling, "let's go greet them!" Car by car all the men got down—and sure enough—four young ladies were there with cotton and needle. Other young ladies would take our arm and zap! We were receiving immunization shots against hoof and mouth disease or something like that. There they called it Mountain fever [Rocky Mountain spotted fever].

Yes, once back in the train, about three hours later, it looked like a hospital. All were crying out, "Ay!" All the men were lying down on the seats. Yes, many of the men, most of them, were crying out in pain and were feverish. Yes, quite a fever! I personally felt the pain, but I did not get a fever. And in both arms—can you imagine! Yes, some were lying down and others had their handkerchiefs around their heads. It was thus that we arrived to this town called, I cannot remember very well what it was called. There we arrived and got down from the truck. Yes, I think it was Lominsula [probably Missoula], Montana. They took us to an office, and the farmers were there waiting for us. The interpreter started talking to us. Well, he would call three, four, one, eight, ten, according to the need of the farmer, according to the work the farmer had.

The farmer was responsible for the workers all the time they were there. It was lucky for us that we got a very nice farmer. He took eight men. We were all from Huecorio. We worked hoeing beets. Since none of us knew that type of work, the *patrón* [boss] went to show us how we should do it. He told us how we should stand so that our backs would not hurt so much. Heck, our backs hurt anyway. By evening time we could not straighten ourselves! And how everybody laughed! Yes, there was so much laughter and teasing. We were all laughing and poking fun at each other. Yes, I am telling you someone would start—"Hey, you lost your step! You lost your step!"

"Well, so did you!" another would answer. Sure enough we were all in the same fix.

The pay? The pay was thirty-five cents an hour. We worked about eleven hours. That's right, by six o'clock one was to be in one's row. We would get up at four or five in the morning to fix our breakfast. We did our own cooking. The little shacks we had, at first glance, well, they did not look like much. They did not look like much from the outside but once inside—well you should see! Very well equipped! They had their grills and heaters inside. No, it did not have a bathroom but the river was close by. And there, in the river, we would go bathing. The restroom—well it was an outside toilet.

We were very comfortable there. We would buy our groceries and there we divided the chores among ourselves. The best one said, "You men get to wash the dishes, and you, over there, you get to gather the wood (our stoves required wood for fuel) and you," he told another, "you be the cook." Others were to make the beds. And it was so that we divided the chores.

After that, we were moved and separated. Afterward, each man bought his own groceries. We would finish a field belonging to one farmer and we would be sent to another field. I cannot tell you, however, if we were under the same contract or if it was another.

Yes, we were there for a while, then, we were sent to Polson, and then, from Polson, we were again moved to Charlo, Montana. And from there, we were sent to Bilos [Billings, Montana].

In Bilos, Montana, we were sent to pick potatoes. And from Bilos, Montana, we were again moved to Charlo to pick beets. Very hard work! We were working with a small machete but we could barely see the beets. Only a small piece, a few leaves can be seen. Then we would grab the small beet ball and yank it out. That is why after two hours of work, our hands were stiff. We could not move them. This happened even though we were wearing layers of gloves: one pair of gloves was made of silk, the other of wool, and the third pair of rubber. It was the same with our feet. We had silk socks—well, the patrón told us what we should wear. He made us wear four pairs of socks and then a pair of shoes and then the overshoes, or boots made of rubber. But even so we were cold, cold. One of the men, he was a funny one, he would say, "Oh, oh, oh, I am cold stiff!" When we got home, we lighted up the grill and he would stick his feet in the fire. He took off everything and would stick his bare feet right in the blazing fire. He would leave them there about three minutes and it was only then that he would feel the fire. Frozen cold! Yes, our feet and our hands would get completely frozen. Yes, it was a very hard life there in that part of the country, there in the snow.

The town, the town was very, very far. That is why we were really roughing it. We did not even have someone to cut our hair. Our clothes were falling apart—and we did not even know how to sew a stitch! All the men kept saying, "What shall I do? I look like an Apache!" We were all day in the mud, you see. We were in the humid, wet earth. We were not clean for very long. And one of the men was nearly in tears because he could not sew his pants. He could not put a patch on them, the way we·do here. One day, I decided to fix my clothing. The men saw me and they said, "Hey, look, why don't you fix mine. I'll pay you." It was so that I made some extra money. And, listen, the haircut, that was even funnier. You see, I bought myself a pair of scissors and hair trimmers and started cutting hair. All the men had nice haircuts except me. I could not cut my own hair! Who was going to give me a haircut? "What am I to do?" I thought. None of the men knew how to cut hair. I finally got two mirrors and placed one in front of me and one in back and there I was by myself, trying to cut my hair. Yes, one does suffer when one is far from a town.

The patrón, he did not want us to go to town. He would ask us, "What do you need?" and he would bring us all our groceries. Yes, the groceries. He did not tell us how much [the groceries cost]

or how [he got them]. At paytime he would deduct from our
wages. But very honest—the patrón. He never cheated us. If he
owed us a penny, he repaid us a penny. Or when we would go to
the stores, when we finally got to go, we would give them money
and they would take out whatever the object was worth. If we gave
them more than it was worth, they would say, "No, this is
enough." They are very straightforward over there. I can vouch
for that.

Yes, I am telling you. Afterward, they moved us to pick potatoes. They paid us by the sack. I got together with an Americano
because there was one of them working there. Between the two of
us, we made good money. One had the sacks belted to his waist
with hooks. The other carried a basket made of wire and that is
how we filled them. We picked the potatoes and filled our sacks.

Between the two of us we made 130 dollars per week. That came
65 dollars per week each. This was different from how we first
started. At first we were not picking potatoes, we were hoeing
potatoes. We hoed for two months. They paid us at that time fifty
dollars per month plus room and board. The food was very good
there at Bilos. The people were very nice. The patrones were very
kind. Yes, they could see that we were hard workers.

One of the patrones really liked me and wanted me to stay
there. That incident happened like this. The patrón had two sons
that were very lazy. One of the sons slept there in the same room
we did. The patrón would get up very early to wake up his son.
"Sonny, Sonny!" he would shake him and call, "Sonny, Sonny!"
and no matter how many "Sonny," "Sonny," "Sonny," Sonny
never would wake up. The patrón would get mad and leave
because it was getting late.

One day, I got up. "Well, this señor, wants some help," I
thought. Well, I got up and went to help him. The poor man and I
were in the same boat—we did not understand what the other
said. He would talk to me in English. I could not understand. I
finally told him using my hands that I had come to help him. He
said, "Okay!" The first day I learned how the work was done. He
had milking machines. He would put some boards on the cows
necks so they would not move or leave. Then he would connect the
machine and start all the machines there. The milk traveled
through a small tube to the milk can and filled it up. It was not
hard to do.

Next day, I was there before the patrón. Yes, I beat him to it. I
said, "I am going to surprise the patrón. He has to call Sonny
first, but I will be over there with the cows."

Yes, that is the way it happened. By the time he got to the cows,

I had already milked five of them. He said, "Oh, *mucho güeno, much güeno!*" (Very good! Very good!) He hugged me. After that he took a liking to me. From then on he really cared for me. He used to call me and asked his wife to serve my food inside with them. And they only invited me. The other men were jealous. Yes, they wanted to know why it was that I was the only one invited to eat with the patrón [and his family] at meal time. I never told them.

Yes, by the time I finished milking the cows, I would go back and the men were barely waking up. They did not know. That is why the patrón and his wife really liked me. They had two young daughters about twenty-two years old and they would go to the fields to help me. Well, with their help I would finish my row quite fast. That is why my friends were mad at me. That these girls only helped me and did not help them made them mad. Well, when we parted—the family cried. I would ask the young ladies, "Why are you crying, Miss?" They did not understand me. They would answer in English and would hug me. Yes, I used to help them sweep and keep the place clean. I made myself useful around there. One day I found a twenty dollar bill. When they got up, I gave it to them. I told them I had found it on the ground. "Oh," the patrón said, "Qué güeno, qué güeno! Tú no echar a la bolsa!" (How nice, how nice! You did not keep it.)

I told him, "No, señor, no." That is why they had so much trust in me. Yes, I really liked it, really liked it. Even though the work is very hard, I still liked it. It is very pretty, over there. Well, it must have been because ever since I was a child I worked in the fields. I do not think it is hard. On the other hand, other men really complain. Over there [in the United States] they used to complain like all complainers because of the work. They used to say, "Heck, I am very tired!" Well, if they did not like it, why did they go? They knew they were going to work. But you know it takes all kinds of people. Some of us see it one way, others see it another way. On my part, I never complained against the hard work. I could see that the reason I had come to the United States was to work. There was no getting away from that. What good was it if one did not want to work or only loafed? One did not eat that way. That is the way I saw it.

On Sundays, that was different. We rested then. On Sundays we went to Mass, we did our laundry. In Millton [Milltown, Montana] this patrón was Protestant—he took us to town. He told us to wait there, to walk around there while he went to his church services. Yes, and as we were curious, you know, we peeked inside their church. Afterward, he took us to our church. They are very fair, yes they are. They do not criticize. Each to his own belief. At least that patrón, anyway. Other patrones did not take us to Mass because oftentimes we went to town on Saturdays instead of Sundays. This was due to the fact that the stores were open on Saturdays and so that we could go shopping and mail our letters. On Sundays, we went back to work.

There [in Milltown] we became friendly with one of those Mexicans they call *pochos*. Those people were nice to us. They used to be our interpreters. They used to say, "Hello, there, do you want to go drink some beer or go shopping? Just call me and I will go with you." He wanted us to buy him a beer or a soda pop in return. He was very happy to be with us and we were more than happy to buy him a beer. He took us shopping. He would tell us how to say it in English or he himself would tell the clerks what we wanted. He was our interpreter, you see. We never had any trouble with them in that state. We never had any trouble with the Americanos either. We were very happy. That Mexican from that state used to tell us that before we came, it had been even better. He would say, "You just got the crumbs!" as we Mexicans are accustomed to saying when we pick the very last, what other people have left. So it was with us. "You came too late, you got the leftovers," he would say. "It was very nice in the beginning because there weren't any Americanos around, only Americanas[2] only patronas. They—the women—used to get together and sponsor dances for the Mexicans, for the workers. They used to make dances so that they would work for them." He used to tell us a lot of those things, you see. That was around '42. By '47 there was not any of that.

Well, at about six months our contract was over. "OK, boys, it's time to go back." They themselves brought us back via El Centro and to Calexico. We were glad to have gone out and seen American soil, but we were glad to see our families and to arrive in good health. I brought home some carpenter's tools. It was hard to bring tools at that time. Many brought pumps to pump out water. No, the government did not do anything at that time. Everything was duty free. Many men brought things like that. Many brought clothes, radios . . . that was the first thing. First, the radio, which was a thing we did not know about here. There weren't any here then—well, there were some but only those that had money owned them. Others brought clothing material, dresses, shirts, blouses.

Others did not even return. They stayed over there [in the

[2]Suffix "as" denotes feminine gender.

United States.] They left the train. They would get down from the
train whenever we made stops at train stations. They would say,
"This is our chance!" They would take to the mountains and who
could find them? Afterward, I thought many times, "What if I
had stayed!" Well, I had my parents. I had my family, my sons
and daughters. You know how many there are that think like they
do. They have a hard heart. They do not care. They go where
they please leaving their families. On the other hand, there are
others that really care for their families. Those who are single, of
course, have no problem. To date there are many of my friends
over there.

I stayed here in Huecorio a few years and by '52 I felt like
taking a little trip back North. In '52, I went to get contracted
again and this time I went to work for a big company in California. This company contracted many braceros. When we arrived
in California, they took us to some barracks where there were
about eight hundred men. In the morning, they would give us
coffee. We would get up at two in the morning. We all would start
waking up and when we got up we would get in line. We wanted
a good place in line so that we could get a good breakfast. After a
cup of coffee we were served beefsteak and eggs, as many as we
wanted. We could have as much as we could eat. We could ask for
one serving and then another. They gave it to you, but at that
hour most of us were not hungry. After I would get my coffee, I
would get some bread, wrap an egg in it, put it in a nylon bag and
I would take it to the fields with me. When I had a breather, I
ate it.

We had to hide when we snacked because the patrón was very
strict about that. He did not even want us to stand up to light a
cigarette. We had to work all day. One day a friend of mine and I
were talking when the field boss came over and said, "Boys, don't
talk. The boss here is very strict. Well, you can talk but don't use
your hands when you do it." You know how we are accustomed to
use our hands when we talk. Those men that had the habit of
smoking, they had to smoke bending down. They would light up
their cigarettes as inconspicuously as possible and smoked them
bent down so that nobody would notice. Yes, they told us that. We
never did know whether it was really the patrón or the field boss
that made that rule. Some field bosses are very strict. That company was the Royal Company and the camp was called Campo
Verde.

Well, by noontime they would bring us huge pots filled with
food and refreshments and everything which they brought in a
pickup. There, when the clock struck twelve, the field boss would

yell, "Lunch time!" and we would leave our hoes and go eat. We would make a circle and one would serve us all. We would get meat with vegetables. It was mostly the same at that camp—meat and vegetables: zucchini, carrots and all that. At the end we got fruit and some soda pop.

Well, we used to get half an hour to rest and during that time we used to play around with the swallows and the doves—birds from the sea. They used to fly near us to eat the leftovers the men had left. Many of the men threw pieces of bread at them. They were quite tame. One time one of the boys that was sitting there said, "How much do you want to bet I'll eat that dove? I'll have it for lunch today or tomorrow."

I told him, "You do not eat those things."

He said, "Yes, I'll eat it!" He took a little rock about this size and he threw it at the dove. Yes, yes, he hit the poor dove. The dove flipped a few times. At that moment, the patrón arrived in his car. He saw the dove flipping around on the ground. Right away he calls the field boss. We kept on working. Next day we boarded the bus. The field boss kept a check list of all the men boarding. Since he knew all of us, he stopped Heraclio [who had killed the dove] and told him, "Heraclio, we are going to move you to another ranch. They need a worker there. Wait here." Very well. We all got in the bus and left. That evening when we returned, when we were coming back, it occurred to me to ask the field boss about Heraclio. I said, "Hey, Don Pachito, what news can you tell me about Heraclio? Where did they transfer him?"

"Hmmmmm," he said, "you won't believe what happened to him. Poor man, he is home by now!"

I answered, "Why was that?"

He said, "Well, didn't you see what he did yesterday?"

"No, we did not see anything. What did he do?" It did not cross our mind that it had anything to do with the killing of the dove.

He said, "The patrón was very angry because he killed the little dove. Here people are very strict about hitting little animals." He continued, "That was his punishment. He is in Mexico by now. Take heed and do not any of you hit any little animal." You know how abundant small animals are over there—we used to see rabbits, swallows, and the deer right near us. They were very pretty. The field boss kept warning us, "Don't even think about hitting the little animals because they are very strict here. You'll have to wait until October—that is hunting season, that is the time to hunt animals—anything you want."

Yes, we were there, working hard. Hurry, hurry, hurry. One

time the Mexican field boss was always hurrying us with his machine. The men on the ground throw up the lettuce heads— in front is the man that cuts them. The cutter goes ahead cutting and putting them on the side. He works bent down with a very sharp knife, and with gloved hands he cuts the lettuce. Well he [the field boss] was really hurrying us. He was right behind us. We thought he was doing it on purpose, that he wanted to run us over with the machine. The men could not keep up with him. They could not throw up the lettuce fast enough to those packing it. Yes, soon we were finished with quite a bit of the lettuce field. [The field boss] just laughed at us.

It was about three days that he worked us very hard, very fast. But no one complained about anything. I suffered because I wanted to. If things got to bothering me or I did not like some- thing, I thought, "Well, no one made me come here by force. I came because I wanted to." As I told you in the beginning, it was our pleasure to come and learn all kinds of things. The ones that did complain were not used to working in the fields. Yes, there in California I learned to work in everything. First of all, the lettuce and secondly, beet work which I knew how to do already. After that, they took us to pick almonds. From there we went to pick onions, then we picked carrots. We learned quite fast how to pick them. It was a matter of cutting the average size ones, the ones that were nice and straight.

From there, we left for San Francisco where we picked flower seeds. We picked about three acres of beets for a Japanese farmer there. That trip was not a very good one for me because in the first place the weather was very bad. We only worked three months there. The weather was bad for about three months. We worked there one, two, three times a week and the rest of the time we were holed up inside because of the rain. It rained a lot one time. So I really did not work much that time.

Yes, that was the time that one of my fellow workers died there. He was a very hyperactive fellow, very eager to show that he was a hard worker. He used to work wearing only his T-shirt and pants and nothing else. And he worked hard. He was so fast we were soon left far behind. He was always ahead of us. Even the field boss noticed him. His name was Lazaro and he [the field boss] use to tell him, "Lazaro don't get too far ahead because the patrón does not want the men to be all spread out. He wants you to be together, together."

"Well, tell them to hurry up," he would answer. He did not pay attention. He was always like that—working very hard. Well, one day he tells me, "Don Pedro, I feel very sick."

"What's the matter?" I asked him.

"I have a fever," Lázaro answered.

I told him, "O.K., do not go to work today. Rest and tomorrow we will see how you feel."

"Yes, yes, I've got to go to work," insisted Lázaro. For two days he worked like that. The third day, he said, "Today I am not going to work because I feel sick."

"O.K., fine. I told you before [to stay home] but you kept saying no," I told him.

Then we left. On our return trip, in the evening, we found him in bed. He was there lying down. I asked him, "Lázaro, how do you feel?"

"I feel sick, after all," he answered. Well, we went to sleep. I told him to take some pills. I gave him some pills, I gave him some water and he said, "Thank you. Go to sleep. We will see how I feel by tomorrow morning."

At midnight, he wakes me up and says, "I want you to call the field boss." I went to him and made him comfortable. He told me, "I cannot move this side." He had no muscle tension. He was completely limp. He still was able to talk but he was limp. I took him in my arms. I sat on his bed and I put him [on my lap] and all he said was, "Do not leave me. Wait until I get well and I will go to your state. I have a great desire to know that area."

"Sure Lázaro, do not worry. I will wait for you," I assured him. A few minutes later I felt his body go limp. He put his head on my arm and died.

Well, we did not even call the doctor. He had not told us that he was really sick until it was too late. He kept it all in. Well, I went to call the field boss and I told him right away what had happened. He was there. He got up and quickly called the doctor. A few minutes later the ambulance came. Afterward, the field boss told us that the doctors had told him the breeze had bitten [Lázaro]. I never heard that before. We thought that over there they throw powder for disinfecting. Yes, it smells there like poison, like the kind they put on [the fields?]. Who knows if he drank that or what, we do not know. But the field boss told us that the breeze had bitten him. The next day, when they were going to bury him, they did not let us go [to the funeral].

(Another [bracero] went berserk from the fright of having a man die there. Yes, the next day, while we were working, he went berserk. He got lost. We did not know, not even the field boss knew what had happened. Either he got lost or he went back to Mexico. Anyhow, he did get scared. He was from the same area. Both were from Oaxaca. This happened in '52 in California.)

Afterward, his folks back home wanted to know what had happened to Lázaro. Well, Lázaro had died there. Another fellow that was also from Oaxaca took care of Lázaro's things. It was a small box, a small chest, but it did not have much clothing in it. It probably had one or two pants, very little. We told him, "You can be in charge of taking this back to his family. You tell them how it was. Because they did not let us go to the funeral. All of us from those barracks wanted to go to his tomb but . . . no. The small town where we were was called Soledad. There, I tell you, we never found out why they did not let us go to the funeral. All we heard was, "He died and he was buried." (Afterward we received a letter asking about the one that went berserk. And that one [the one that went berserk] we knew nothing about his final whereabouts either. We did not know anything. Yes, sad. That was all we saw.)

We spent all day in the field working. We would get home tired. Afterward, we had supper and then we went to sleep. Because we had to get up at two o'clock in the morning. So when we came home at night, we wanted to rest, to take a bath. Yes, we would come home full of dirt and very tired. On Sundays we went to Mass.

Sometimes other local growers would come and ask, "Hey, boys, any of you want to work on Sundays?" Well, many of us went, so that meant we did not go to Mass. They would pay five dollars an hour. Yes at five dollars an hour we really made money. What we did was pick almonds. They would hand us a big blanket which we would spread underneath the tree. They would also give us a steel rod and there we were hitting the almond tree with the steel rod. (How we ate and ate the ripe ones!) By twelve o'clock the farmer would come honking his car or pickup. He would bring in the food. He would yell, "Lunch time! Come and get it!" Naturally we would eat all the food. There was lots of food. Besides we were full of almonds. After we ate, we would get a pack of cigarettes, a pack of matches. At the end of the day he would tell us, "I'll see you next Sunday!"

It was not long before someone told our patrón that the workers were going out on Sundays [to work for other growers.] Yes, the patrón was angry. He said that if we wanted to work on Sundays, he too had work [for us]. He had given us Sundays off so that we could rest. After that, the local farmers would come to ask us and we told them no. We told them, "No we cannot work anymore. You see, these people here do not want us to work for someone else. They might send us back to Mexico and that would not be funny. Or perhaps if you have work, after our term expires here, let us know. We will not leave.''

The farmer answered, ''No, I cannot promise that. They will get angry at me here,'' he continued, ''no, what I want is volunteers, but if you cannot work, then let it be. Then I realized that because the farmer had not sold his product to the company, the company did not let him [use us as] workers.

Well, our contract ended and I came back to Mexico. But I did not last long here in Mexico. Life is very hard and once we know the way, we are always thinking about it.

By 1953 I felt like going back to the United States and again I did go. This time I went to get my [bracero] contract in the city of Monterrey, Nuevo León. First, I went to Morelia where they issued a letter of recommendation. Then in Monterrey we were taken according to a list they had. There were times when there were no orders [to take us.] We did not get to go according to the list posted but two, three, four [days] or a week, two weeks or a month, a month and a half later. Meanwhile, we waited in the camp where the contracts were issued. Sometimes, we did without food because we had not brought enough money. Sometimes we could work there. We could work two or three days in the steel factories or beer factories or in some other industry because that is the type of work they have there. But we were always wondering whether our name had come up. If there was still a week before our name came up, well then, we went back to work.

Sometimes when our turn came, they would give us lunch and would tell us to come at seven o'clock at night to get our ticket so that we could travel by bus or by train. We needed our draft card, or if we did not have that, we needed a letter of recommendation and a certificate from the capital of the state from which we came. We could prove our age by means of the draft card because there were some who changed their names or did other tricks so they could go.

At that time, I was sent to Reynosa and crossed the border at Hidalgo. There, we were to serve our contracts in Arkansas. We left September 8 from a small town called Niopol [?]. We were to work picking cotton. There, I worked for a really nice patrón. He was a very good man. The one that was kind of strange toward the workers, [however], was the field boss who was of Mexican origin. He would insult the workers. He treated us really badly. He was one of those Mexicans born in Texas. The Americano was a really nice man. He treated us very well. At lunchtime he would bring us fruit, soda pop, or other things. Every day he would bring us milk.

The field boss was the one who was not always friendly toward us. Yes, he was a mean man.

As time passed and it was evident that the patrón and the field boss did not get along, they fired the field boss. One of the fellows from San Pedro [Coahuila], who was well known to us, he was the one that was made field boss. He, too, was a bracero but he got the job because he was the oldest among us. We were all young.

Well, be that as it may, this patrón, in order to encourage us to work harder, would give out shirts as prizes. The fellow who picked the most was the one who got the prize. Keeping the prize in mind, we would pick very hard hoping to get the shirt at the end of the week. We were paid three dollars per hundred pounds of cotton the first picking, the second picking was $3.10, and they kept increasing the amount to four dollars, that was it. I would usually make 18 to 20 dollars a day. However, some of the other men would not make as much because they would pick only 250 pounds or [less].

Then winter came. We were then sent back by bus. When we [arrived at] two big cities [with a] river between, they asked us at the office if we wanted to work some more, that there was more work available for those that wanted it. We told him yes, but that the weather was very cold. He said no, that it was a matter of working in the ranch or if the work was in town, that winter clothing would be given to us. We said yes, that we were happy to work. After that, the patrón came. He told us the work was going to be in San Antonio, Texas. [In San Antonio] it is not as cold, it is a milder climate and it is easier to work.

We worked in San Antonio from November 27th to February 24th. We worked in the cabbage. It is the custom to plant a lot of cabbage in that area and also carrots. Afterward, [we worked] fumigating and later picking carrots and still later picking radishes.

[Next they took] us to Hidalgo, Texas, [where] they renewed our contract. They took the other one away and threw it away. They gave us some work there in a small town called El Gauch [Edcouch, Texas] near Elsa.

Well, we worked there with a patrón—I do not recall his name. We were working there by about February 27. We worked planting cotton. We were separated in twos. Each rancher got two [braceros]. Another fellow from Morelia and myself worked together.

They had us planting there. We were given a mule attached to a small wagon and we rode it in a straight line so that it was pushing the soil down where the cotton seeds were. That way, the cotton seeds would be deep enough so as not to dry up. Well, we worked there. After some time the field boss told us if we wanted to rest we could, that we had fifteen days left and if we wanted to work for another patrón we could. He would grant us permission. He was going to pay us anyway. We told him, "Well if you give us permission to work, very well."

We worked for another [farmer near Mercedes, Texas] who had a herd of cows. Then, you see, since I am a curious fellow, and I knew about sickness in animals (I grew up on the farm), I saw that the field boss there was not taking care of the cows. (I had started to get near the animals, to see if I could help milk the cows. I was hoping that they would give us some milk for breakfast. He said yes, that we could have milk every day. All we had to do was go for it. One day when I went for milk the field boss was there not knowing how to cure a bull, which was the stud bull. It was a great huge gray Brahma bull. He asked me what we should do with this animal. I said, "Well, the question is what do *you* do with it? I only came to watch."

"Don't you know anything [about animals]?" he asked me.

I said, "Yes I do, but what if I make a mistake? You are going to say why did I stick my nose in something that was not my business!"

The field boss said, "Well, if he dies, it must have been his turn to die."

I said, "If you let me take care of that animal, he will not die." We made a wager there. He asked me how much I had, how much money I had. I answered, "I only have seven dollars."

"Well, double your money or nothing," he said.

"O.K.," I answered.

"But let's not tell the patrón," the field boss cautioned me. It was just a conversation we had there, you see. Then, I rolled up my sleeves to cure the bull. Well, in about fifteen minutes the bull was up and around eating as if he had never been sick. He had gotten sick with the alfalfa he ate. It is bad for them when it is wet with dew. It is bad for animals.

After that the field boss started disliking me because the patrón would call me to look at the animals. The field boss himself was the one that told the patrón that I was the one that had cured the bull. It was his own fault. Why did he tell the patrón? He should not have told him. He should have said he had cured the bull. No, he did not do that. He told the patrón I had cured the bull.

Then the patrón started noticing how intelligent I was. So he started having me work closer and closer to the ranch house. The month of May came, that is when the sun is really strong. All the other men were out in the fields hoeing, cleaning up the weeds, others hoeing cotton. The cotton was growing tall at about twenty centimeters. The animals were constantly getting sick. The patrón would send for me, would get me from the fields, you see, so that I could look at the animals. Sometimes, the animals would die before I got there because I would not get there in time.

Well, in the month of June, when the cotton was ready for clipping, the cotton bolls were large, ready to have the points taken off, you see. Because some of the cotton plants were really growing tall, we would cut the tops with a machete. It was at that time that one of his cows died. I was only about 300 meters away but no one told me. The field boss was trying to cure them. You see, he wanted to feel important. He used to watch me trying to see how I cured them. He did not do anything for the cow. The patrón came and was very angry with the field boss because he had let the cow die. He went to call me but I said, "What for? The cow is dead! It has already died!"

After that the patrón fired the field boss and left me in charge as field boss. I was in charge of taking care of the animals. I was to look after them. The ex–field boss would give me dirty looks because he was out in the fields working and I stayed. Each morning, since he was the one that drove the pickup, he would take the men out to the fields, then bring me to the stable so that I could care for the animals. That was what really made him angry. You see, I was only a bracero who was not authorized to be head man. That was not to his liking. But the patrón was only interested in having his animals taken care of by me. When I was there, I quickly cured them.

After that, the patrón wanted to get my legal papers so that I could work there permanently. But at that time, I wanted to come home and see my family. I did not want to stay. This was around July, around the 24th of July in '54. You see I left in '53 and came back to Mexico in '54. The cotton was ready to burst and the bolls were ready for the first picking. That was when I got a letter from Mexico urging me to come home. They wrote that my mother was sick and wanted to see me. The patrón said I could take out a fifteen-day permit to return to Mexico. He told me that if I wanted to, he would grant me the permit so that later I could come back to help him. He said he did not want me to leave him, to leave his work because he was very happy with me.

Well, it was done so. We arrived at Hidalgo and he took out my permit and I came home. I stayed fourteen days in Mexico, then I returned. The day I [returned to the United States] was a Sunday and I was not allowed to cross there in Reynosa. I telephoned the patrón and he went to Hidalgo and crossed the border to Reynosa.

He wanted to know what had happened. I told him I had not been allowed to cross because it was Sunday. He said, "O.K., I will give you some money so that you can go to Monterrey. In Monterrey, see if you can get a contract to come here with me. Anywhere you cross, if it is Piedras Negras, or if it is here in Hidalgo, I will come for you so that you can take care of my animals." He said, "I can do no more."

I said, "Very well." He gave me fifty dollars so that I could return. That is why I went to Monterrey. I stayed there about fifteen days but I could not get a contract. I needed a certificate from my local government. I did not have it. It so happened that a priest was there in Monterrey. We would have a talk with him and he would help the men go through. Afterward, the men would give him a donation for his church, as if nothing had happened, you see. He would call the camp, he would call the chief giving contracts there in Monterrey. That time, I got my contract again but I was to cross at Piedras Negras.

I tried to telephone my old patrón but they did not let me. They said no, that if we worked for the same patrón we wanted to become United States citizens. They said it had to be with whomever happened to need people. So that is why I could not return there [with the same patrón].

On that trip I met up with a fellow from here, from Michoacán. The other men were all strangers, almost all were from border towns. We worked picking oranges. After that we were picking lemons and from there we went out to cut bananas which were near the coast of a large body of water. We never knew what [the name of that body of water] was but there was a lot of water there. All around that coast we cut bananas. They told us that those bananas grew wild there, that no one planted them there.

After that, we went back to picking oranges. The oranges there were huge. We were paid by the pound. One cent per pound of oranges picked. We used to make about thirty dollars per day. The only thing was that we only worked two or three days a week. We did not work the whole week. We could only work two or three days because it rained a lot. When it rained we could not work because of it. You see the cars would get stuck in the mud and could not come out. So we could only work three days and that was it. That was the reason we could not make much, because of the rain. When they saw that we were not making much in two days a week, they took us back to the Association[3] to see what could be done with us.

[3] Bracero processing office.

From there, we were sent back to El Paso. We asked them if we could work in something else. They said no, that there wasn't any other work. We told them, "We do not have any money because we had bad weather. We could not work because the weather was bad."

There an official made a telephone call to the consulate and asked if we could stay at least fifteen more days. Well, they took us to pick, to pick carrots around there. We were not making much money there either. We only made three or at the most four dollars a day. Yes, the times we made four dollars that was the most.

After that we went to pick onions. You see, the tractor goes into the field and plows the onion out of the ground. The men go into the fields with a pair of big scissors cutting the tops and the roots, leaving only the onion and dropping it in small bags. We were paid twenty-nine cents a bag. Well, we really had blisters on our fingers. We would cut the onions but since the onions were full of mud, soon the scissors were not able to cut at all. So we spent half of the time cleaning the scissors so they could cut and sharpening them with a file. The men were only making four dollars, or five dollars per day, at the most.

Some days we would only make twenty-five cents. We were only able to pick one single sack of onions. It was not because there was not any work, the reason was rain. It was during the rainy season around the end of November, of December. During those months one is unable to work because the rains come. Sometimes there is fog, the breeze, you know. And very fine droplets of rain. Then we cannot work. Sometimes, the weather is good but by tomorrow a heat wave comes.

The weather is quite variable there in Texas. Sometimes the days are nice and then suddenly bad weather comes. And then the North winds come. Even if it does not rain, when the North winds come and hit you, you freeze to death by the time you get to the field (or the "cuadro" because in Texas they call it "cuadro" and, in, huh, California, they call it field).

Well, that time we were there, the field boss told us that it was not worthwhile for us to work there, that we should ask for a change. We said, "Well, if we only have fifteen days to work so that we can make enough money to pay our passage back home, what we want to do is work. We want to work every single day left. What are we going to gain by moving about?" Some men do ask to be moved. I did see that when they asked to be moved, they were sent back to México. When do they make it better for you in a job? They cannot!

Well, anyway, be that as it may, they let us work for fifteen days plus an additional week. Because times were pretty hard then. That time that we were leaving for Mexico, then in Hidalgo, a man who was a cattleman asked who knew how to castrate horses and who knew how to castrate cattle. I immediately raised my hand, "Over here, hey!" What I wanted was work. I did not want to come back to Mexico, I wanted to work, in anything. I wanted to earn money. Right away, they separated me. There was another fellow there also.

"What can you do?" asked the officer there.

"Well, I know how to cure animals of this and that," I answered. Well, I told him all I knew there.

"Where did you learn? Here in the United States?" the official asked me.

"No, I learned in Mexico," I answered.

"How old were you?" asked the official.

"Since I was a lad," I answered.

"How many days do you want to work?" the official asked me.

I said, "As many as you can give me. If you give me a lot of days, fine. If you only give me a few, well whatever you say." Well, right away they took me. They renewed my contract to test me whether I really knew or not.

I do not remember the name of the ranch but it was right there in Texas by the border, between MacAllen and Edinburg.

Well, there they had that type of "masked" cattle. The one that has a red body with a white head. It was all cattle there. The cowboys were there with their lariats, roping the animals. There I arrived. You see there are many ways one can castrate animals. I did not know how to castrate them with a knife. I knew how to castrate them by pulling on them. Therefore, they really liked it. You see, that way none of the animals die. You see, by using the knife the cattle become infected, they get worms, they have a hard time, they get skinny and look pretty bad. So there I was all day castrating animals. Yes, as they were left there ready for me to do my job, it was not hard for me. I did not use up my strength. I just got them there where they were tied up. I did not have to use up my strength.

The Americanos had never seen animals castrated the way I did it and they thought it was funny. They would laugh. I had to tie [the animals] as soon as they were ready with a piece of string so I could tell them apart [from those not castrated]. They had to wait three days to untie them. Well, the animals soon were healthy, they were not sick because they do not lose their appetite. They keep eating. They do not get skinny. [And] I managed to work longer because I told them which animals were O.K. and which animals were not. Well, they gave me fifteen days. At about the twelfth day I went back to the corral where the cattle were. All were fine except for a young calf. It was the only one that had not come out all right. The animals had not gotten skinny at all. Not one of them.

I used to tell them there that they should get me a contract. They said they did not have any other work for me. The days I was there, I spent about four days castrating and the rest of the time, I was picking watermelons. All the watermelons that were in one of the fields, I was asked to pick them. They paid me five dollars a day for picking watermelons and ten dollars for castrating.

Soon, another patrón wanted to have his animals castrated. He had liked my method and wanted me to teach him. I went there. I could not teach him! I used to tell him how to do it and no, he could not do it. He could not do it because they are not used to hard labor. He would tire very fast. Also, I had learned since I was a boy. They wanted to learn fast; to do it fast. You cannot do that. You have to be waiting, fixing them there for awhile until they are done. He could not learn in the days I was there. Some were not castrated right and I returned to castrate them and to cure two that were sick and another that had bugs. These bugs appear in lumps that come out in their belly and their back, or their neck. It is a very contagious disease. Then, he told me that I had to castrate I think 194 bulls. I told him if he had more, I could do more. I went and in three days they were ready. [To thank me,] he gave me a pants outfit—all that comes in an outfit. He took me to Hidalgo and I did not get another contract there. They sent me back. But they were very pleased.

Well, I did not return that year. I came back to Mexico and when I got home I worked here.

The year 1956 came along and there were more contracts. This time in Guaymas, Sonora, or nearby Empalme. I did not want to go that way because it was very far, one needed money to go. I did not want to go because I was afraid it was going to be hot. Be that as it may, I managed to get some money. I went to Morelia first to get my certificate. I got the certificate and the government's list and I left. This time they sent me to Blythe, California.

There in Blythe, it was precisely the fourth of September, I arrived and there was this heavy rain falling. They were picking cotton there. I considered myself one of the best cotton pickers, but over there it was a different type of cotton, pima type, that type that has small balls. Well, they took us to the field, and they gave us the sacks and—on to pick! We hit it hard! Well, it was not long before we were halfway down the cotton row and we did not even have half a sack picked! I told myself, "I'll never get through here!" Yes, we would hit hard and pick fast but the sack was still empty. I said, "What are we going to do? We are not going to make much here! Let us really hit it hard!" And we would pick harder. We would finish the row and come out to the end of the row and we did not even have half a sack. "No this is not going to be worth our while," we thought. And we did not even know how much they were paying.

Well, it was Wednesday when we started working. Thursday they took us again to the same field. That day I picked about thirty-eight pounds, I think. I did not even get my sack full. That cotton really was like nothing. The cotton balls were very small and quite stuck. We would pull at it and not get much. We had to pull twice so that the whole ball could come out. But we still did not get much.

By that week, I think I got about eleven dollars. I did not make enough to pay room and board because that was twenty-seven dollars. So I did not even make half of the room and board. The following week, on Monday, they asked, "How is it there?"

"No, it is not any good. Let us go back to Mexico."

Well, I never like to follow the crowd. I do not like to be around crowds. I like to be by myself. Then all the men were in a crowd yelling, "Strike!" and "This is no good!" and "On to Mexico!" I let them do whatever they wanted. I did not stop.

Then, the field boss came, "What is it, boys? Are we working?"

"No, it is not any good!" and "Strike!" and "Strike!" I was sitting over on the side with two other fellows.

"And you? What about you? You are not going to work?" he asked us.

"Yes, we are waiting for the bus to take us." We answered.

"Well, let's get to work," he told us. Well, no one wanted to go except three of us from about a total of 197 men. From 197 only three men went to work. They took us to the same field there. We had not finished it. Well, we started to work there. We were very happy, talking with each other. That is why we had come to work. What business was it of ours to look for trouble?

That afternoon when we came back [to the camp], there was no one left. They had moved them. Well, they had not really moved them, but had sent them back to Mexico. After that, it became better for us. You see, the next day they took us to work on the cantaloupes. We had to pick the cantaloupe vines up from the ground and place them on top so that the tractor's tires did not run over them and kill them. So we were there, the tractor behind us while we were up front lifting the vines. Well, slowly not fast. By noon, the field boss came and brought us lunch and said, "What happened to you?"

"Nothing, we are doing fine," we answered.

"All right," he said, "tomorrow you will go work for another man. Only you three. We do not have any more men in the camp."

We said, "Fine, that's good."

The field boss said, "You were the only ones not fired."

"No, we did not run. We came to work. We did not come here to be lazy. We work anywhere as long as there is work," we answered. Well, he immediately took us to another farmer so that we could work in something else. But they told us there was not anymore work. We told them, "We do not have any money. We have had a bad time." Then the official telephoned the consulate and we were granted fifteen more days. They said yes, that we could stay. They took us to work nearby. That week I worked planting lettuce. All week I planted lettuce so that when it came out it was transplanted in Salinas.

The following week I worked only about two hours, for which I was paid. Well, I worked for such a short time that I did not even make enough for room and board. I kept wondering where I was going to get the money to pay for it. I did not want the money to send home. I wanted to pay for the food I had been eating. That was foremost in my mind.

Well, the patrón with whom I was working asked me if I did not run [from work]. I said I did not run. That I had come to work and did not run. So he took me to Rio Colorado, the one that flows in California and Arizona. He asked me if I was afraid. He told me we were going to go get some fish. That he knew how to fish. He had a small boat and he took it to fish. Well, I liked it. He told me he was going to pay me by the hour. He said that if we worked two hours he would pay me two hours or if we worked the whole day, up to fourteen hours, I would be paid the fourteen hours. Well, O.K. It was really great for me because I knew how to fish, and we caught some [big ones] with fishing hooks. We fish here in Lake Patzcuaro [so] I knew how to fish by an easier method without as much danger to us [as the method he wanted us to use]. There were a lot of gunny sacks, the ones they use to store seed, potatoes or sweet potatoes, well, bulbs like gladiola bulbs (because they plant a lot of flowers over there). Well, we gathered all those sacks and made one big sack out of them so as to make a fishing net. In order to use them we placed stones on them. It took me about a day and a half to make that net. We used the ropes found there to make the net. We went fishing that same afternoon and we fished for about two hours. We threw in a lot of pieces of bread. We threw bread down and put sand on top so that it would stay down and then the fish could get close to eat. (The water there is very calm and everything goes to the bottom.) Then we would go and place the sack around. After two hours we had so much fish we did not know where to put them. I had worked very well. Well, he liked [my work] and I stayed there more than two months with that Americano. Then he told me he did not have any more work for me. He took me back to the Association.

My contract was renewed and I went to Salinas to pick lettuce. They paid us $1.05 an hour and we worked fourteen hours. Sometimes we worked twelve or ten hours but we worked constantly even on Sundays. By the 25th of December, the field boss told us that he did not have any more work for us; that the cold weather was coming.

Well, they sent us back to Mexico. I wanted to come home anyway. You know how sometimes you feel like going back to one's family. We came home and the relatives start asking you, "Well, how was it?"

"Fine," I answered.

"Which state did you like the best?" my family asked me. I told them that I liked California the best because we can earn more money and there is more work but the treatment, the way the patrones treated you, was best in Montana and Arkansas.

"And the Americanos, how did they treat you?" my relatives wanted to know.

The Americanos treat us very well. The ones that treat us bad are the Mexicans. Yes, the Mexicans that are born over there. They felt resentment against us. It is because they feel bad. They should defend us. They feel uncomfortable with us. Yes, it is one's own kind who treat us badly. They try to take advantage of us. We tell them something and they pretend they did not hear us. They laugh instead at us. Everything they do is like a game to them. On the other hand the Americano, one talks to him, one tells him this or that and he takes it very nicely, [for example, when] one gets sick. . . . I got sick over here in Texas. You see one day I fell from a cotton trailer. I emptied my sack full of cotton and as I was getting down, I slipped from the ladder because it was wet and I fell, ladder and all. In a few days I started to feel a little sick, I was not feeling right. Well, I called the field boss to see if I should go see the doctor. Anyway, the insurance was paying for it. Well, he started laughing. He took it as a joke. I was just telling him. Well, that Saturday in the afternoon at paytime I told the patrón. I told him, "Listen, I want you to know I feel sick and if I continue to feel this way, in a few days I am not going to be any good for anything, not even work. I would like you to take me to see a doctor."

The Americano said, "Sure!" He left the payroll there, the money he was going to pay and he took me to see the doctor. Right away the doctor prescribed some capsules and I was soon well. In five days I was well again.

Well, I told my family about the different peoples that were there in the United States. I had never known the Chinese before nor the Italians. I thought they would look different but when I became acquainted with them, well, they were a very friendly people, very reasonable. All people are the same but I imagine that the Americanos are the nicest. Yes, the ones that are of American origin because there are many other peoples there, you see, but ones that are legitimate [Americans] I think are most reasonable. Because in California there are many patrones who are Filipino or Greek, I think, I do not know what kind of people they are. Over there in Cocha [Coachella, California] I worked with Italians.

The ones that glared at us were the Japanese. I had this Japanese patrón and he was very stubborn and a hard worker. Because they are the hardest-working people, more than any other. Well, we are good workers but they exceed common sense. As soon as the clock strikes six o'clock the Americano says, "Let's go!" You leave everything behind. The Americano is not distrustful. The Japanese is very distrustful. He thinks someone is going to steal something that he has around his place. Heck, why should one take his things! And the Americano is not distrustful at all. He leaves everything there, even his truck, the one he would drive to pick us up, he would leave there.

Here, life is very hard. The times I went to the United States, well, each time I went, all the money I earned while working there, my family saved it here. It was all well invested. Since I have stopped going, I see that we are always limited in funds. And I think that if I went over there again, that if there was a chance to work, if I could get documents so that I could go, I think I could have it easier here. Because, here we do not make much. The only way is to go [to the United States] or to start some business. The reason I have it halfway decent is because I have been raising chickens for about four or five years. If it were not for that, I would have long ago taken off even as a wetback, to the United States. Yes, there couldn't be anything else to do. We go out to work here in Patzcuaro and they do not pay you anything.

The government does not protect the farmer here at all. I don't say [that banks should give money away], but they should charge one percent interest. That is a good amount for the bank. But they charge eight percent! That is the profit they make. That is what I am talking about when I say one cannot get involved with the bank. I did business with the bank. They charged me eight percent annual interest. In the end I paid fourteen percent annual interest! So you see, they never live up to the contracts they write. So where is one to end up? If one does not pay them, they keep adding up, adding up. And that is what I see wrong here in Mexico. Now, if one goes to talk to a lawyer, "Sir, this has happened to me and I need some help."

"Yes, but it will cost you this," they answer. All it is, is pure robbery, pure robbery is what they do.

[Or if] one goes to ask a favor from an official, anyone of them [they ask], "Who do you know? Bring me X amount." Well, if one is unable to identify oneself with the documents one has why should there be any reason for someone else to identify us? You see all they are trying to do is get their "mordida" (bribe) as we say here in Mexico.

I used to hear that there was a lot of "mordida" that the bracero had to come up with so that he could go to the United States. They would ask some braceros for 1,000 pesos and 500 pesos were asked of others. Still others were asked 300 pesos. Well, one official asked me, "Do you have something?"

I said, "Well, no, I do not have money. I only have [my place on] the list. The top official there issuing out the contracts was the same, stretching out his hand [asking for money].

"Oh," he says, "if you do not have any money you wait until Monday. If you want to get through, try getting some from the other braceros here.' "But they are in the same boat I am. They did not bring anything. I do not care what day I go through as long as you keep the list active."

On Monday the list was called and they sent us inside to register us. You see the doctors checked you to see if you were healthy or if you had some type of disease. Once we are in the United States, they spray our head with DDT because they must think that we are full of lice or something else. But [the United States] is where they have a lot of lice, now that I remember. There in San Francisco we got infected with lice just because we went into a second-hand store.

By the way, I once met one of those Texans, one of those rude ones. Yes, he was a touchy one. If we were not standing in a straight line, you see, he would get angry. He was the only one that [way]. I was there with a friend [and] we could not even talk. If they tell you come here or this is all for today, then that is the way it is. And yes, they would pick you here, and you, you, and you and that is it. We did not have anything to say about the whole matter. We go because we are eager to go over there, to work, to be sure, to earn money. I wanted to travel in the United States because everybody tells you here, "Ohhh, it is very pretty." And this and that. "And you get to earn a lot of money!"

[Once] I went to Canoga, California, and I was almost dying there. In the first place let me tell you, I do not have a queasy stomach. The thing that happened, however, was that the change in food was what got to me. You see in the first place, that little ranch where we were sent, the cook, a so-called man named Chale, well, all he gave us was two fried eggs and about two pieces of bread and fried potatoes. I could not digest them very well. Now, the lunches, well since he was alone with his wife, you can imagine what a hard time they had trying to feed about seventy individuals. Our lunch consisted of two tacos made with flour tortillas with some beans and some fruit and that was all. To boot, we did not even eat them when we were working. We thought that maybe he was seasoning them with something to make them taste good, maybe that he added some vinegar or something, but it was not that. They were giving us spoiled tacos.

After a while, I started, then others too, we were not eating our tacos. Out in the field, where we were working, you could see the whole tomato field blanketed with white. Everywhere you could see the white spots. You see we were throwing our tacos away. And since we were picking tomatoes, you see, many would eat tomatoes and the fruit that came with our lunches. We did not complain to anybody. We did not know what they were doing but we just did not eat them. I finally got stricken with a terrible case of diarrhea. I think the food caused me to get sick.

Well, I tell you, there in that ranch we could see the tacos strewn all over. The love of money makes you do anything so nobody said anything. I think it was about forty-five days that we spent mostly running to the bathroom. It was a good thing that at the end of the forty-five days they moved us to another patrón.

Here in this other ranch, supper consisted of coffee with cream and about two pieces of bread. How foamy were those darn pitchers! One day we happened to be there when they were filling the pitchers with water and adding powdered milk to them. We never drank milk after that!

In San Fernando, I really had a bad case of diarrhea. But in that case it was again, as we say here, because we were so timid, so lacking in words, you see. I told myself, "Well, if I tell the patrón he might get angry and say 'Do not work a few days.' One is so eager to work, to do one's chores. I tried to see if I could sweat it out, but I continued to be sick.

But there in San Fernando the food was a little better. However, if we wanted to eat, by five o'clock we had to be in line. They served us boiled eggs, or fried eggs or anyway we wanted them. We got a cup of oatmeal or as many as we wanted and that was our breakfast. At lunchtime we got four tacos. They were really good. They were made with different fillings: green beans, meat, beans and we also got a small carton of milk with a piece of fruit. At night, for supper, we got a really good supper. We would have chicken soup or beef stew—good supper! We were very happy there. The housing consisted of tents, army tents, that is what we called them. We were very comfortable with two blankets and two sheets.

Sometimes we went to town. One time a really funny thing happened to us. You see, when we went over there we had our hats, as you know we always wear our hats. Well, one time we stopped at this store in Canoga and the men there would yell at us: "Puro Pancho Villa!" because of the hats, you see. Right away they could tell we were from Mexico. In the first place we were very shabbily dressed and secondly our hats. Well, we stopped at a secondhand store, where they sell used clothes, you see. We started to buy some shirts there and would you believe, the man there, the clerk there, he was a gringo for sure because he did not speak Spanish well. Anyway, he liked one of our friend's hats and he proceeded to take it away from him. Our friend had taken it off and set it aside and when he wanted to get it the man told him that it was not his. He said it was not his and there was nothing we could do. We said to ourselves God only knows what they will do to us here.

We left, and we left very angry because of the hat, but we left anyway and we never returned because we had just arrived and who knows, maybe they would have called the police. If we had thought the thing through, that the police couldn't have done anything to us if he had called them, how could they ever have thought the hat belonged to the man there? But, I tell you, we were afraid knowing we were in another country. We had just been there five days. We could not say anything. We got out of the store and we teased our friend, "Hey, you lost your hat!"

After that I was sent to Santa Ana, in the county of Oranch (Orange County). Work there was pretty good. I worked there quite a bit, I can truthfully say that. I would go in at four o'clock in the morning—at five at the latest. I went in to work early because my job was fumigating the tomatoes. I carried this little machine with which I did it. Yes, it was like a little can and it had this container. I would put some powder in it and so I had to go to work early. After eight o'clock, I would stop doing that because the temperature would start going up; I would quit because it got hot. The powder gets in your eyes and when it's hot, ohhhh, your eyes sting very badly, very badly. And someone had asked me before, "How much are they paying you there?" I do not remember who asked me, "How much do they pay you there?"

I told him, "Well, they pay us a dollar an hour."

He says, "No, for that type of work, that wage is not right. That type of work should get you at least $1.10 per hour. Work requiring fumigation, working with [insecticide] powder should pay more."

I told him, "Well, here they pay everybody the same; a dollar an hour."

"No," he says, "That is not right. You should complain to the Association."

I told him, "No, what for. I have just arrived here and if I am a trouble maker they will soon throw me out [of the country]."

There, the work was pretty good but our food was pretty bad. The food was just awful, awful. There was this lady, who by the way, was a Mexican lady, an immigrant herself, who was mean of character; yes, her personality was very mean and, well, we were about fifty Mexicans that she had to feed. Actually there were about seventy-five men around there. They had Japanese men there but the Japanese had their dining room in another section. A Japanese cook did their meals. They did not mix. They were always together. At work we would mingle with them, but for their meals, for sleeping, they were apart from us. They slept in different barracks and there they had their dining room. Their bathroom was separate too.

When we Mexicans came to eat, we had to be there at exactly the right time because if we were a tiny bit late: "Well, you are the last one. There is no more left. I do not have time to be waiting for you. . . ." Nobody would answer her. She would send us our lunch, a couple of sandwiches with only some bologna or wieners. Heck, we did not like that. Not a single taco did she send us. Only sandwiches with bologna and wieners. Sometimes an orange, but most of the time, nothing, nothing. The board was really bad. Sometimes we would go to a restaurant to eat what we wanted.

The medical treatment [was also bad] there, the doctors did not care about us. For any [ailment] we had we were prescribed pills, pills, that is all. Yes, only pills. One time I do not remember what was wrong with me, I do not remember what was the matter with me, if it was my stomach or my head, but I told the patrón, "You know, I feel rather sick."

"What is the matter?" he asked me. Well, I told him where the pain was and he said, "All right, in a few minutes they will take you to the doctor." There were patients there with different ailments, right?

We got there and entered to see the doctor.

"And what is wrong with you?" he asked.

"Well, I have this," we would tell him.

Some men were more ill than others. Still others were not as sick. When we went out, we asked each other, "What did the doctor give you?"

"See, this little gift? Some pills. And you?" someone would ask.

"Well, I only got some pills too. And you?" another bracero would ask.

"Well, I got some pills too," yet another bracero would say.

"Well, do we all have the same illness? What is this?" one of the braceros would ask.

"Who knows," we said.

All pills! Others would go and the same, pills, and they were the same kind too. Maybe if they had been different or been given a different dosage, right? No, we would check out the pills and the same. "What effect did it have on you?" we asked each other.

"Nothing, I feel the same," we would answer.

It was only when someone was seriously ill, like with a serious operation, I think, then they would do something. A fellow from here from Huecorio died in a Yuma camp. When one comes out here one is testing one's luck. Some win, some lose. A man never knows if he will return to Mexico. During the later years, the Americanos were really behaving badly. It was then that they said Mexico was going to stop the bracero program.

Well, I served my contract that year and when I came back I had a radio, a sewing machine, and a suitcase, a small one, not too big, full of clothing. I also had a hair trimmer and all kinds of carpenter's tools. Well, they opened it [the suitcase] there at the border on the Mexican side, there in Sonorita. They wanted me to give them a fifty peso bribe and then they would let me pass. I told them that I was not going to give him anything because I had paid for [the suitcase] with my money. I was not going to give them anything! "It is stolen," the customs officials told me.

I told them, "I have not stolen anything. I have my receipts here, look. Everything I have here, I have bought." Finally, I took out a five peso bill so that I would not keep people behind me waiting. There was a line there. Five pesos I gave them. But they really wanted to take away a watch that I had there. They wanted to take it away because they said that was the only thing that would cover the import tax.

The whole thing is shameless thievery, nothing else. [Once upon return to Mexico], I had a suitcase with clothing and I had an electric radio. I was with some other fellows from here from Morelia. There was a customs agent there that kept tugging at the radio and asking me if I had a gun. I told him, "I do not have one but if I did it would have been because I bought it."

The customs agent says, "You have to pay fifty pesos."

I told him, "I wish I had them so that I can eat. I spent all my money on these things. So I do not have anything. The little I had left, I sent to my family." I told him, "I am not going to give you anything because I have the sales receipts." Well, we did not pay attention to him, and another fellow, those that are really tough, who was with me, he did have a gun and he told the customs official, "I do have something, I am telling you before you search me. Let us through." And in so saying he pointed the gun at the official's stomach. "Let us through. I do have one—that is why I am showing it to you. I do have a gun!" And he showed the gun. He pointed it at him. They let everybody pass! They did not charge anybody that time. Yes, that fellow was the one that scared him by his "I do have one." He told him, "I'll use it on anyone who is against my bringing it, like you. I think I will use it on you!"

On the other hand, in the United States I remember one time that they searched me. I had a knife and they took it away from me but they threw it in the wastebasket. They also took away the knife from another fellow but I did not know that it was against the law to carry a knife over there. I carried that knife with me so that I could use it to slice onions or for any other chore that I might need it, like cooking, or other types of jobs. They thought it was for fighting, for cutting someone. But I cannot say they took anything else from us or say that they wanted money; no, nothing, nothing.

In the latter years, getting a contract was very hard because there were a lot of people that wanted to go. So one time I took a chance and went as a wetback. We crossed the river via Arguellas, Texas. Well, we were soon caught by the immigration officials. They caught us while we were picking cotton. They did not even give us a chance to get our few articles of clothing we had, though old they were. They just made us board the bus they had and took us. There, they asked us questions, you see. They wanted to know where we were from and how old we were. They wanted to know if we were married and how many children we had. Well they asked us a lot of questions like that and then they sent us to Reynosa, [Mexico]. Three days later we crossed the river again. No, they would not even give you a chance to get your clothes.

I ventured out for three years. One time I paid forty dollars to cross the river but after that, I never paid again. The other times I went, I knew the way. Why I even helped other fellows cross the river by swimming across it. We found a patrón and we worked for him a while. He used to take care of us and he did not let us go to town. Heck, we had trouble understanding. One time we went to the post office and we asked for an airmail stamp. No, he could not understand us. Finally we made gestures with our hands, using them as if they were wings. "Stamps, like this!" and they laughed, but they understood. We did have a hard time because we did not speak English.

The truth is that life is very hard here [in Mexico]. Some days we have work and there are others that we do not. Wages are the lowest. When harvest comes, a worker lasts one month harvesting the corn, the wheat. Wages were seven pesos before, now they were paying ten pesos, but I tell you, it is not sufficient to live on. Corn costs about three pesos, 2.50 pesos, 2.85 pesos around there. He who has two or three in his family cannot make it; cannot do it. But if we go over there and you get some good luck, well, yes. And here the money is more. Here one dollar is 12.50 pesos. When one is working over there you really have to have bad luck to get caught. You know the immigration over there is everywhere. I was really astonished the first time when we were picking cotton and an airplane arrived and was circling above. Well, we threw ourselves on the ground, you see. There nearby was an orange grove with thick grass growing. Well, many took off. We left the sacks we had and we ran into the orange grove. Well, we stayed there. Heck, it was not long before the pickup truck came. The immigration officers came and there they were kicking the cotton rows [looking for people]. Yes, they caught us. We used to laugh at ourselves because we hid under this dike that was there by the canal and we hid there. One of the immigration officials that spoke a little Spanish said we looked like rabbits because we had hid there. "Out you go!" he said.

Sometimes, they are mean. They start kicking you and they

have this stick and they twist your arms with this leather that they have. And they take you to the car like that. Well, that time they threw us out.

But life gets so hard here in Mexico that is why one takes a chance. Sometimes I do not have work and there I am searching around. That is why I want to be over there to earn a few dollars. Many come back here with good cars, those that are legal residents over there [in the United States]. Naturally it is another way of life. Over there you can buy a car for fifty dollars. Yes, a car worth a thousand dollars is really something over here. Over there [in the U.S.] you talk in the hundreds, over here [in Mexico] you talk in the thousands. [You can buy a car in the U.S. for $200-$300. In Mexico you need thousands of pesos.] I would like to go buy one. I would also like to buy some tools that would be useful to me. Things one cannot get here. That is why I am interested in going. Since I have to leave money for my family, I cannot do it. But I am interested in making another trip there.

Comment on Pedro's Story

So far we have seen very different views of the bracero experience as depicted in Mexican fiction and a composite oral history interview with the bracero himself. We have seen that for the most part the experiences in fiction described by the elite were generally unpleasant, traumatic, and degrading. In several cases the image of the bracero portrayed in the works was that of a money-hungry, greedy, discontented individual ready to humiliate himself for the "almighty dollar." In other cases, he was ridiculed for his attempt at becoming "Americanized," and in still others, he was a pathetic figure unable to survive in a hostile and exploitative universe. The bracero, on the other hand, saw himself as a man conscious of what he was doing, aware of the dangers and sufferings that awaited him, but imbued with ambition nevertheless, going about life with an adventurous, inquisitive, conquering spirit. No matter what lay ahead of him in this strange, alien country known as the United States of America, he knew he could survive with less exploitation than in Mexico.

3
The Bracero Experience in
Folk Song

Given the differing views portrayed in the first two chapters, how has the bracero's image been consecrated in song, a major means of communication among braceros themselves?

One of the most common forms of folk songs used is the *corrido*. The corrido, as experts such as Vicente T. Mendoza, Américo Paredes, Merle E. Simmons, and Arthur L. Campa agree, traces its antecedents to the old Spanish romances which were introduced in America in the early days of the Conquistadores. It is an extremely popular form of expression as well as a source of entertainment for the Mexican peasant and for other members of the lower classes of society. Its easy rhyme and meter lend themselves to any theme and are readily mastered by the composer who generally is not highly educated or trained in music. In other words, the corrido is a form of musical expression written for the people and by the people and containing themes relevant to the people. In its more classical narratives it has achieved epic proportions for it immortalizes the deeds of its heroes. Such corridos as "Benjamín Argumedo," "Pancho Villa," "Corrido de Zapata," and "Valentín de la Sierra" are well known to most Mexicans. The corrido has proved to be easily adaptable to a wide variety of themes and thus we find them written for almost every occasion: those dealing with horses, with some type of catastrophe, with tragic events, and so on. It is thus that we find the bracero experience depicted in the lyrics of the corrido.

Vicente T. Mendoza defines the corrido in *El romance español y el corrido mexicano* (1939) in terms of subject matter:

The Mexican corrido is in essence a lyrical genre, primarily narrative, which narrates with a simple and invariable musical phrase composed of four members those events that powerfully touch the sensibility of the masses; violent crimes, violent deaths, tales of bandits, catastrophes, railroad derailments, wars, battles, heroic deeds, humorous stories, simple love couplets, couplets of unrequited love, or of a satirical nature. As can be seen, it includes the epic vein of battles and heroic deeds that give origin to the heroic *gesta*.

The diverse titles by which the corrido is known in Mexico are: *romance, tragedy, exempla, corrido, verses, couplets, tale,* etc. This diverse manner of distinguishing it derives from the subject matter treated and not from its musical forms (pp. 118–119).

Some of the first corridos collected in Mexico revert for subject matter to battles and heroic deeds as in the traditional Spanish romances. The rebirth of the romance in the form of the corrido was no doubt stimulated by the many wars and political conflicts of the turbulent years that followed the Independence movement of 1810 in Mexico. As Mendoza puts it in the same work quoted above:

It is the wars, the revolutions, the riots, and the *coups d'etat* that have given rise to the songs of war, the camp ballads and the corridos in which shall be consigned the deeds, the defeats and victories of innumerable heroes (p. 131).

The corrido proved to be a popular and easily adaptable musical form of expression and during the turbulent years of the Mexican Revolution of 1910–1917 the corrido peaked in creativity and popularity.

An earlier study done by Merle E. Simmons entitled *The Mexican "Corrido" as a Source for Interpretive Study of Modern Mexico (1870–1950)* (1957) tangently touched upon the bracero and his attitudes toward the United States. In Part Four of this book under the heading "Relations with Foreigners" Simmons analyzed the "pueblo's" (common people) attitude toward the "gringo" as expressed in the corrido. This corrido scholar detects a strong anti-Yankee sentiment up until the late 1930s. He states:

It comes as no surprise to anyone who is familiar with the Mexican scene that the *corridos* reveal profound dislike and even hatred to be the basic traditional attitude of the Mexican *pueblo* toward the United States and North Americans. Indeed, in treating this aspect of the Mexican mentality, chronology is of little significance until World War II. There is no apparent evolution of attitude—only peaks and depressions in the vehemence of the masses' animosity (pp. 420–421).

Most of the antipathy toward the United States expressed in the corridos deals with the military intervention of the United States into Mexican territory. Episodes in the corridos which show strong hostility to the United States refer to such historical armed conflicts between the two nations as the Mexican American War of 1848 ("Las Margaritas"), American occupation of Veracruz in 1917

("La heróica acción del capitán Azueta" [The Heroic Action of Captain Azueta]), General Pershing's expedition undertaken in 1916 in search of Pancho Villa ("La persecucion de Villa" [Villa's Persecution]), and the fear of military intervention during the oil expropriation era of the 1930s ("Corrido petrolero" [The Petroleum Corrido]) among others.

The corridos with bracero content collected before 1935 showed an ambivalent attitude toward the United States: some portrayed the positive gains made from working in the States while others zeroed in on the ill-treatment Mexican workers received from the Americans known popularly for their big feet. Most of these corridos with negative bracero experience content are associated with the more significant protest made against North American military intervention as stated earlier. Some examples follow (all references are to Simmons, 1957):

In "Los ambiciosos patones" (The Ambitious Big-Footed Ones), the complaint is (p. 427):

Insultan a los mexicanos	They insult Mexicans
y los corren de los campos,	And run them off the fields
para ocupar a sus paisanos	So that they can hire their
que llegan como lagartos.	countrymen
	Who arrive as alligators.

In "La llegada de buques americanos a Tampico" (The Arrival of American Ships in Tampico), they say (p. 428):

En los Estados Unidos	In the United States
linchan a los mexicanos	They lynch Mexicans
y los dejan sin trabajo	And they leave them without
porque son muy inhumanos.	work
	Because they are very inhuman.

And in "La triste situación" (The Sad Situation) we hear (p. 429):

Se pasan Mexicanos pa'l otro lado	The Mexicans cross to the other side
creyendo que son [the North Americans] formales,	Thinking they [the North Americans] are straight-forward,
y allá tan mal que los ven	And there they are mistreated
los ingratos federales.	By the ungrateful federal authorities.

All corridos from Merle E. Simmons, *The Mexican Corrido as a Source for Interpretative Study of Modern Mexico (1870–1950)*, are reprinted by permission of Indiana University Press (Bloomington, Ind.).

Ah! qué ingratos Patones!	Oh! What ingrates those Big-
ya a la gente vuelven loca,	Footed Ones are!
metiéndose por los ranchos	They drive the people crazy,
y llevándolos en troca.	Going into the fields
	And taking them in trucks.
Luego que ya los agarran	After they apprehend them
les hacen observaciones,	They are placed under
por caminos y condados,	observation
esos ingratos patones.	On the road and in the counties,
	By those ingrate Big-Footed
	Ones!
Los llevan a Emigración	They take them to the
los sentencian a la Corte	immigration office
los que van de contrabando	They sentence them in court
aunque lleven pasaporte.	Those that go by contraband
	Even if they have a passport.
Pobrecitos prisioneros	Poor prisoners
que a la Corte van a dar,	Those that end up in court,
a tomar agua caliente	They will drink hot water
y luego avena sin sal.	And later oatmeal without salt.

Another corrido dating from the 1890s collected by Américo Paredes, "Desde México he venido," warns braceros of hypocritical U.S. politicians. Finally, in "Los emigrantes" (The Immigrants) we hear (p. 429):

Mas hoy con la nueva Ley	But today with the new law
del Gobierno Americano	Of the American government
por donde quiera es mal visto	Everywhere [they] are mistreated
todo pobre mexicano.	All poor Mexicans.
Porque los Americanos,	Because the Americans
no nos tienen compasión,	Do not have any compassion
y hombres, niños y mujeres	for us,
los llevan a la prisión.	And men, women and children
	Are taken to prison.

Corridos narrated from the point of view of one who has been in the United States tell a different story. A positive attitude is ever present in those corridos wherein the narrator implies he has been north of the border or is about to go there. In "Las pollas de California" (The Chicks from California) the humor which will be a constant in the later corridos collected after 1936 is most evident (pp. 436–437):

Bonito California	Pretty California
donde gocé de placeres,	Where I enjoyed many
lo que no me gustó a mi	pleasures,
que allí mandan las mujeres.	What I did not like
	Is that there the women rule.

Las pollas de California	The chicks from California
gastadoras de dinero,	Like to spend a lot of money,
para salirse a pasear	When they go out
piden guantes y sombrero.	They ask for gloves and hat.

Las pollas de California	The chicks from California
no saben comer tortilla,	Do not eat tortillas,
lo que les gusta en la mesa	What they like on the table
es el pan con mantequilla.	Is bread and butter.

And in "Los norteños" (The Northerners) a future bracero exclaims (p. 438):

Los gringos pagan muy bien	The gringos pay very well
y son muy considerados,	And are very considerate,
aquí no he de trabajar	I will not work here
con los ricos hacendados.	For the rich "hacienda" owners.

Still another bracero dreams about the great and prosperous times awaiting him in the States as seen in corridos such as "El cuándo de los estados" (The "When" of the States), "Los braceros" (The Braceros), and "Los planes de un bracero" (A Bracero's Plans). The corrido "Consejos a los norteños" (Advice to the Northerners) is typical of these (pp. 441–442):

Ahora sí van a lonchar	Now you will be lunching
y a comer buenos jamones,	And eating good ham,
porque aquí en nuestro terreno	Because here in our land
no compran ni pantalones.	You cannot even buy pants.

Vamos a Estados Unidos	Let us go to the United States
a ganar buenos salarios,	To earn good salaries,
que los señores patones	Because the Big-Footed people
necesitan operarios.	Need workers.

Vamos a portar chaqueta,	Let us go wear jackets,
lo que nunca hemos usado,	Which we have never worn,
camisas de pura seda,	Pure silk shirts,
como también buen calzado.	And high quality shoes as well.

Aquí, si nos afanamos	Here, even if we work hard
siempre andamos encuerados,	We are always naked,

por allá en el extranjero
parecemos diputados.

There in that foreign country
We will look like congressmen.

¿Qué dicen amigos vamos,
por allá es la pura miel,
se toma buena cerveza
y se come en el hotel.

What do you say friends?
  Shall we go?
Over there it's pure honey,
One can drink good beer
And eat in a hotel.

¿Qué dicen? gorras de maíz,
no quieren usar tejano
los convido a trabajar
con el gringo americano.

What do you say, corn hats?
Don't you want to wear a
  Texan hat?
I invite you to work
For the American gringo.

No crean que soy pretencioso
ni tampoco fanfarrón,
de trabajar muy barato
me duele mucho el pulmón.

Do not think I am a show-off
Or a braggart either,
From working so hard
My lungs hurt me so.

Aquí no hemos de hacer
  nada,
tómenlo por experiencia,
porque el dinero se esconde
por nuestra falta de ciencia.

Here we will not make
  anything
Take it from my experience,
Because money evades us
Because of our lack of science.

Adios, muchachas hermosas,
adios todos mis amigos,
regresaré de Fifí,
portando muy buen abrigo.

Good-bye, beautiful girls,
Good-bye all my friends,
I will return very Fifí [high
  class],
Wearing a fine coat.

This idealized view of the bracero experience was ridiculed through the lyrics of corridos such as "Los deportados" (Deported) and "Los norteños" (The Northerners), which tried to demolish so "exaggerated" a view of the U.S. experience (pp. 442-443):

Ya llegaron los Norteños
del punto de la Frontera,
todos vienen presumiendo
que son la chucha cuerera.

The Northerners have arrived
From the border,
All come bragging about
How rich they are.

Porque ahora traen pantalón
ya se creen que son catrines,
se fueron patas de perro
y hoy presumen de botines.

Just because they wear pants
They think they are dandies,
They left barefooted
And now they sport fancy boots.

Muchos hablaban tarasco,
pero hoy pronuncian el YES,
mas no saben otra cosa;
son puros patas de res.

Many spoke Tarascan,
But now they are able to
    pronounce YES,
But they do not know anything
    else;
They are really a coarse bunch.

The bracero is not to be intimidated, however, for he delineates in a caustic manner the reasons for leaving his country in the corrido "Defensa de los Norteños" (In Defense of the Northerners) (pp. 444–445):

Lo que dicen de nosotros
casi todo es realidad;
mas salimos del terreno
por pura necesidad.

What they say about us
Is almost all true;
But we leave our land
Through sheer necessity.

Pero la culpa la tienen
esos ingratos patrones
que no les dan a su gente
ni para comprar calzones.

The fault lies
With those ingrate bosses
That do not give the people
Enough to buy pajamas.

El rico en buen automóvil,
buen caballo, buena silla,
y los pobrecitos peones
pelona la rabadilla.

The rich have a good
    automobile,
A good horse, a good saddle,
And the poor peons
Ride bareback.

Yo no digo que en el Norte
se va uno a estar muy sentado,
ni aun cuando porte chaqueta
lo hacen a uno diputado.

I do not say that up North
One goes to sit and relax,
And even if one wears a jacket
One does not become a
    congressman.

Alli se va a trabajar
macizo a lo americano,
pero alcanza uno a ganar
más que cualesquier paisano.

One goes to work there,
Hard, American style,
But one is able to earn
More than any of our
    countrymen.

Aquí se trabaja un año
sin comprarse una camisa;
el pobre siempre sufriendo,
y los ricos risa y risa.

One works here a year
Without buying a shirt;
The poor people always
    suffering;
And the rich laugh and laugh.

Ansia tenemos de volver	We are eager to return
a nuestra patria idolatrada,	To our beloved country,
pero qué le hemos de hacer	But what can we do
si está la patria arruinada.	If the homeland is ruined?
Que no vengan de facetos	I entreat my fellow workers
les digo a mis compañeros;	Not to return all a-bragging;
amigos, yo no presumo,	Friends, I am not a show-off
porque soy de los rancheros.	Because I am a farmworker.

Simmons correctly intuits the change in feeling in the pueblo toward the United States in the years to follow. The beginning of the Good Neighbor Policy instituted by President Franklin D. Roosevelt in 1933, the coming of World War II which found Mexico on the side of the Allies, and finally the great influx of braceros coming to North American soil in large numbers and finding out firsthand what the United States was all about contributed to the change in feeling. Corridos of the early thirties describe the pride in coming to work in the United States. Simmons cites three corridos that portray these feelings of pride and self-worth on the part of the Mexican worker: "Soy bracero Mexicano" (I Am a Mexican Bracero), "La despediada de los braceros" (The Braceros' Farewell) and "La despediada de los reenganchados" (The Farewell of the Re-contracted Workers). An example from "Soy bracero mexicano" follows (pp. 453–454):

Soy bracero mexicano,	I am a Mexican bracero,
he venido a trabajar	I have come to work
para esta Nación hermana	For this sister country
que me ha mandado llamar.	That has called on me.
A mi país piden brazos	They [the U.S.] ask for arms
para poder substituir	To substitute
a los que están en la lucha	Those that are fighting
sin el temor de morir.	Without fear of dying.

Simmons's intuition about the change in Mexican attitude toward the United States proves prophetic as can be verified upon reading the lyrics of the corridos below.

The sixteen corridos with bracero content treated here deal with the post-1935 era up to the present, an era of extremely high Mexican immigration. They can be divided into four major categories depending upon the general theme and tone: (1) "Proud-to-be-Mexican," 50 percent; (2) the bracero experience satirized, 19 percent; (3) the homesick, nostalgic bracero, 12 percent; and (4) bracero protest songs, 19 percent.

The bracero folk songs have not been systematically set down. It was difficult to locate even the sixteen songs studied, some of which are published here for the first time. More are continually being composed.

The general tone of most songs dealing with what might be considered the sensitive subject of bracero life is humor. In this respect the corrido and other forms of folk song are more in accord with the sentiment of the bracero himself than with the elite interpretation in fiction. The underlying themes, however, deal with the sufferings, exploitation, difficulties, and hostilities that the bracero worker has experienced in the United States. Thus, although some of the experiences depicted are harsh, the harshness is deflected by the humor injected in the corrido. The overall attitude toward the bracero experience found in these songs lies somewhere between the stance taken by elite writers in their fictional works and that expressed by the bracero himself. That is to say, in the elitelore of middle class intellectual writers, the bracero experience is viewed as an abominable one; in the lore of the bracero, the experience is seen as a challenge and adventure; in song the experience is depicted as harsh but funny.

Let us examine the folk songs dealing with the theme of the bracero, today's undocumented workers.

"Proud-To-Be-Mexican" Songs

The older corridos dealing with immigrant themes, found in Vicente T. Mendoza's *Lírica narrativa de México: el corrido,* portray the Mexican immigrant as an extremely proud, self-confident individual. The corridos were mainly collected in the years 1936–1953, which were the years before the main bulk of the fictional short stories and novels were written.

The corrido "De 'el interior' o de 'Los enganchados' " (Mendoza, 1964:38*b*), collected in 1936, portrays a happy, cheerful, optimistic campesino on his way to the United States. His optimism of a better life in the United States leads him to invite his girl friend to accompany him: "Let us go to the United States, we shall be happy there!"

De "El interior" o "Los enganchados"

—De esas tres que vienen áhi, ¿cuál te gusta, valedor?
—Esa del vestido blanco me parece la mejor.

—Ya ven, deja de moler, ya no muelas nixtamal,
vamos a Estados Unidos, que allí iremos a gozar.

—Oyes, ya, chinita, el tren; oye qué silbidos da,
nomás un favor te pido: que no llores por allá.

—Querido, ya me cansé y apenas aquí es Torreón,
pa'el cansancio no sentir cánteme *usté* una canción.

¡Qué canción tan *reteflais,* que jamás la había *oido* yo!
Cánteme otra más bonita y después le canto yo.

Ya le dije al *enganchista,* le dije que volvería;
pero que no venía solo, ahora traigo compañía.

From *"The Interior"* or *"The Contract Laborers"*

"Of those three that are walking by, which do you like,
    troubador?"
"That one with the white dress seems to be the best."

"Come now, stop grinding, stop grinding corn.
Let us go to the United States, we shall have fun there."

"Do you hear, my love, the train? Listen to the whistle blowing.
I only ask one thing of you: do not cry over there."

"My loved one, I am tired, and this is only Torreón.
To relieve my weariness, sing a song to me."

I have never heard such a crazy song, I had never heard that!
Sing me another, prettier one, and then I will sing to you.

I told the one who signed us up that I would return,
But that I would not come alone. I have company now.

A corrido written in 1936, "Del viaje de la 'Típica de Policía' a California" (ibid., p. 396), deals again with the proud Mexican eager to go to the United States. In this corrido the Mexican worker is aware of his own worth and views himself as a good-will ambassador to the United States. He is an extremely nationalistic Mexican, wishing to spread the good word about Mexico. He is going to tell the people of the United States about the great things that can be found in Mexico, its beautiful cities and fantastic music. The bracero happily states: "Our beautiful music we want to spread and our virile songs will speak about our race!" These are the songs, according to the Mexican immigrant, made by "men of the Revolution, sired without fear." The "Típica de

Policía'' probably represents a musical group, like the police bands
found in so many villages in the Spanish-speaking world.

Del viaje de la "Típica de Policía" a California

¡Adiós, México querido, testigo de mi alegría!
Me mandan a California con mi "Típica" querida.

Yo ya me voy, te digo adiós,
voy a cantar las canciones/del pueblo trabajador.

El día dieciocho de julio llegamos a la Estación,
el tren ya estaba formado y había "cuates" de a montón.

—¡Quihúbole,/pues! ¿Pa' dónde van?
—Nos vamos a California nuestros sones a cantar.

—¿Adónde vas, Miguel Lerdo?—me dijeron mis amigos.
—Pos ya se los dije, cuates, voy para Estados Unidos.

—¿Qué vas a hacer? —Ya lo sabrán,
dejaremos bien plantada la bandera nacional.

"Diré a los americanos lo que es mi México hermoso,
donde hay trabajo y contento y el pueblo vive dichoso.

"Yo se los digo y es la verdad,
que México es muy hermoso y es tierra de libertad."

—¡A Estados Unidos salen!—nos dijo mi general—,
quiere el señor Presidente que vayan a trabajar.

—¡Ándele, pues, jálenle ya;
muchachos, lo ordena el Jefe, por algo lo ha de ordenar.

Nuestra música preciosa tenemos que propagar,
y nuestros viriles cantos por nuestra raza hablarán.

—Le damos, pues, me canso ya;
ya le estamos dimos dando, comiencen, pues, a afinar.

Huapangos, sones, valonas, del Bajío y de Michoacán;
y los "sones socialistas" que alientan para luchar.

¡A poco sí! ¡Cómo no!
Canciones de hombres sin miedo que dió la Revolución.

Si lejos de nuestra tierra la suerte, los trata mal,
¡vénganse, pues, camaradas a México a trabajar!

¡No sufran, más, *jalen pa' allá!*
Pa' que sepan lo que vale tener Patria y Libertad.

About the Trip of "Típica de Policía" to California

Good-bye my beloved Mexico, witness to my happiness!
They are sending me to California, with my beloved group.

I am leaving, I bid thee farewell,
I shall be singing the songs of the hard-working people.

On the eighteenth of July we arrived at the station,
The train was ready to go and there were "brothers" all around.

"Hey, hello! Where are you going?"
"We are going to California, our songs there to sing."

"Where are you going, Miguel Lerdo?" my friends asked.
"Well, I told you, brothers, I am going to the United States."

"What are you going to do?" "You shall soon know.
We shall leave a good image of our national flag.

"I shall tell the Americans about my beautiful Mexico.
Where there is work and happiness and the people are contented.

"I tell you this, and it is true,
That Mexico is beautiful and is a land of liberty."

"To the United States you go!" the general told us.
"The President wants you to go to work."

"Come on, get going; boys, the Boss tells us so.
He has his reasons for doing so."

Our beautiful music we want to spread,
And our virile songs will speak about our race.

"Let's get going, I am getting tired.
We're on our way, start to tune up."

Huapangos, songs, valonas from the Valley of Michoacán,
And the "socialist songs" that inspire us to fight.

It is true! Yes it is!
Men of the Revolution, sired without fear!

If far from our land, luck will treat you badly.
Return to Mexico, friends, to work.

Do not suffer, go over there,
So that you know what it means to have land and liberty.

The third corrido in this category, written in 1953, is entitled
"De 'La maquinita' o de 'El emigrante'" (ibid., p. 383). The
main tone of the corrido is that of an excited adventurous bracero.
The corrido reads like a travelogue as the bracero describes the
scenery as he travels on his way to the United States, adventure of
travel being underscored. We hear about San Luis Potosí,
Aguascalientes, Zacatecas, Torreón, Gómez Palacio, Parras, Chihuahua, and Juárez which are situated on one of the main routes
traveled by the braceros coming into the United States. This
particular bracero came to work on the railroad tracks.

De "La maquinita" o de "El emigrante"

¡Corre, corre, maquinita; corre por esa ladera!
Parece que voy llegando a orillas de la frontera.

¡Adiós, parientes y hermanos! ¡Adiós, todos mis amigos!
¡Quédense, adiós, ya me voy a los Estados Unidos!

Salí de San Luis Potosí con rumbo de Aguascalientes,
¡adiós, todos mis amigos! ¡Adiós, todos mis parientes!

Al pasar por Zacatecas vi todos sus minerales,
que desde el tren *se devisan chorreaderos* de metales.

Al pasar por El Torreón me dijo una *chimolera*:
—Mañana sale el *enganche,* ¿qué dice, señor, me lleva?

—No, señora, no la llevo, porque tengo a quien llevar.
Y hasta lloraba la ingrata que no se quería quedar.

Pasé por Gómez Palacio, vi el Río del Tlahualilo,
(que) riega los algodonales de San Pedro y de El Higo.

Desde allí se *devisa* Parras de la Fuente,
donde hacen muy buen vino y también buen aguardiente.

De Parras pasé a Chihuahua hasta que llegué a Juárez,
y al día siguiente salí a visitar sus ramales.

Trabajé en el "Traque", me dieron mi provisión;
desde allí me *juí* bajando Estación por Estación.

About "The Little Machine" or "The Immigrant"

Run, run, little machine, run through those farms!
It feels like we are getting nearer the border.

Good-bye relatives and brothers, good-bye my friends!
I take my leave, good-bye, I'm going to the United States!

I left San Luis Potosí headed toward Aguascalientes,
Good-bye my friends, good-bye my relatives!

While passing through Zacatecas, I saw all its mineral richness.
You can see even from the train the glitter of metals everywhere.

While passing through Torreón, a young "chick" told me,
"Tomorrow the enlisted crew leaves; will you take me with you?"

"No, my dear lady, I cannot take you, because I have someone
    else already."
And the poor girl cried and cried for she did not want to stay
    behind.

We passed through Gómez Palacio, I saw the Tlahualilo River,
Whose waters irrigate the cotton fields of San Pedro and El Higo.

From there you can see Parras de la Fuente,
Where good wine is made and good firewater.

From Parras we passed through Chihuahua and then we arrived
    at Juárez.
And the next day I went to visit the local sights.

I worked on the railroad line, they gave me groceries.
From there on I stopped at every station.

"De 'El traque' o de 'El lava-platos' " (ibid., p. 376), collected
in 1948, can be seen as a transitional corrido for it contains both
aspects: the excitement and adventurous spirit of the traveling
bracero and the satire that will predominate in the corridos that
follow it in the 1950s and 1960s. The corrido narrates the story of
a young man who dreams about becoming a movie star. He therefore decides to go to "Jolibud" (Hollywood). There, instead of
finding "fame and fortune," he finds himself in the lowly task of
washing dishes! A friend tells him about work available on the
railroad and our bracero, believing this to be a department store,
finds himself in a roomful of dirty dishes. His next job is not much
better for he finds himself on his knees picking tomatoes and
hoeing beets.

After this arduous work, the bracero decides to go to Sacramento where he finds work on a construction site. All of these misadventures are told with tongue-in-cheek humor making use of the double meaning of words to provide the comical effect.

The last eight verses leave the play on words and hard work aside in order to describe another traveling route, this time on the United States side. The traveling bracero describes cities and states such as St. Louis, New York, Detroit, Alaska, California, and Texas. He finally bids the listener good-bye saying he is returning to Mexico to see his Mexican girls and because of his love for his "Julia."

De "El traque" o de "El lava-platos"

Soñé yo en mi juventud ser una estrella de cine
y un día de tantos me viene a visitar *jolibud* (Hollywood).

Un día, muy desesperado de tanta revolución,
me pasé para este lado sin pagar la inmigración.

> ¡Qué vacilada! ¡Qué vacilada!
> Me pasé sin pagar nada.

Al llegar a la Estación me tropecé con un *cuate*
y me hizo la invitación de trabajar en "El Traque."

Yo, "El Traque", me suponía que sería algún almacén;
y era componer la vía por donde camina el tren.

> ¡Ay, qué mi cuate! ¡Ay, qué mi cuate!
> ¡Cómo me llevas pa' "El Traque"!

Cuando me enfadé de "El Traque" me volvió a invitar aquel
a la pizca del tomate y a *desahijar* betabel.

Allí gané indulgencias caminando de rodillas,
haciéndoles reverencias tres o cuatro y cinco millas.

> !Ah, qué trabajo tan mal pagado
> por andar arrodillado!

Mi cuate, que no era maje, él siguió dándole guerra
y al completar su pasaje se regresó pa' su tierra.

Y yo hice cualquier *bicoca* y me fui pa' Sacramento;
cuando no quedó ni *zoca,* tuve que entrarle al cemento.

¡Ay, qué tormento! ¡Ay, qué tormento!
es el mentado cemento.

Echéle tierra y arena a la máquina batidora a
cincuenta centavos hora hasta que el *pito* no suena.

Recorrí pueblos y villas, todo aquello es un primor;
pasé por San Luis *Misuri* y llegué a Nueva York.

A Ditroi, Míchiga fui, ciudad de los automóviles;
visité sus maquinarias, ¡ay, qué bonito, señores!

Me pasé al Polo Norte, vi sus grandes pesquerías;
vi las focas y gaviotas que yo no las conocía.

Me pasé a California, vi sus grandes naranjales,
y vi sus grandes plantíos de grandes *jitomatales.*

Bonito Estado de Texas por su grande agricultura,
pues tiene muchos plantíos, todo es una hermosura.

Los gringuitos me decían:—¿Te gusta lo que aquí ves?
Era de los mexicanos y ahora de nosotros es.

Adiós, los americanos, también las americanas,
quédense, adiós, ya me voy; voy a ver mis mexicanas.

¡Bonito Estados Unidos, que no me quedó ni duda!
Me vine de por allá por el amor de mi Julia.

About "The Railroad Worker" or "The Dishwasher"

I dreamed in my youth of being a movie star,
And one fine day I came to visit Hollywood.

One day, desperate from all the revolutions,
I crossed to the U.S.A. without paying the immigration:

What a joke, What a joke!
I crossed without paying a cent!

Upon reaching the station, I came upon a "brother"
And he invited me to work for the "Traque."

I thought "El Traque" was a fancy department store,
But it was fixing the rails where the trains run.

What a "brother"! What a "brother"!
How you took me to the railroad tracks!

When I got tired of "El Traque" he invited me again
To pick tomatoes and to hoe beets.

There I earned indulgences crawling on my knees,
Bowing down for three, four, and five miles.

What poorly paid work
For working on one's knees!

My friend, who was no dummy, he stuck to it,
And when he had his fare he returned home to Mexico.

I worked for almost nothing and left for Sacramento.
When I had nothing left I had to work on the cement.

What a horrible torment! What a horrible torment!
That so-called cement.

Pour some dirt and sand into the cement mixer.
Fifty cents an hour all day 'til the whistle blows.

I traveled through towns and cities, and is all such beauty.
I went through St. Louis, Missouri, and arrived at New York.

I went to Detroit, Michigan, the city of the automobile.
I visited the assembly lines, how beautiful it was!

I went on to the North Pole; I saw all its great fisheries.
I saw all the seals and swallows, which I had never seen.

I traveled on to California and saw all its orange groves
And all the huge tomato farms.

The beautiful state of Texas with its huge agricultural farms
Has many crops; all is very beautiful.

The "gringuitos" would ask me, "Do you like what you see?"
It used to belong to the Mexicans, now it is all ours.

Good-bye, American men, good-bye American girls.
I take my leave, good-bye, I am going to see my Mexican girls.

The United States is beautiful, there is no doubt about that.
I had to return home, because of my love for Julia.

Another "happy to be traveling" song of the "proud bracero"
is "Chulas fronteras" (written and recorded by Eulalio González

in *Ajua con "El Piporro,"* Gas Records 4081, side 2). Here the bracero is depicted as a strong, intelligent, self-confident man who gets the best of an Anglo "Sheriff." The Mexican here, as is common in Mexican jokes, manages to portray the "gringo" as stupid, clumsy, or idiotic. The self-image of the Mexican in most folk songs like this one sharply contrasts with the image that most North Americans have of Mexicans. In his songs, the Mexican sees himself as a strong, macho type who is also clever, witty, and intelligent. Actual braceros generally share this same image. Thus the popularity of the song.

Chulas Fronteras

HABLADO   Chulas Fronteras del Norte como las extraño. No las miro desde hace un año.

CANTADO   Andándome yo pasiando
por las Fronteras del Norte
¡hay que cosa tan hermosa!
De Tijuana a Ciudad Juárez
de Ciudad Juárez Laredo
de Laredo a Matamoros
sin olvidar a Reynosa.

HABLADO   Me acuerdo la primera vez que fui a United States of America.
—¡Qué no me fui a pasiar, me fui a pizcar!
Le escribí a mamá, "Amá ya compré saco."
Una argüenda que armó mi mamá: "¡Mi hijo anda muy bien vestido. Trae saco nuevo!" ¡Nada, pos el saco de pizcar!

CANTADO   Una muchacha en el puente
blanca flor de primavera
me miraba me miraba.
Le pedí me resolviera
si acaso yo le gustaba
pero ella quería otra cosa
¡le ayudara en la pasada!

HABLADO   Me vio fuerte de brazo ancho de espaldas, me cargo de bulto. Y yo haciéndole tercera. Al llegar a la aduana me dijo el de la cachucha "¿Que llevas ahí?"
"Ja puro *wiskle.*"

"Pos si pero llevas cien cajas!"
"Es que ando de parranda y no soy de botella—¡Soy
de caja! Agarra dos pa' tí." Y no las agarró. ¡Se
quedó con todas!

CANTADO   Antes iba al otro *lao*
escondido de la gente,
pues pasaba de mojado.
Ahora tengo mis papeles
ya estoy dentro de la ley
tomo whisky o la tequila
hasta en medio del highway.

HABLADO   En eso llegó el Cherifón. Un pelao que me saca
como dos metros de alto. Y nos vimos cara a cara,
bueno eso de cara a cara es un decir. ¡Lo más que
le alcancé a ver es la hebilla del pantalón!
"Hey tu Mexicano, ¿Tu eres mojado?"
"Wait a minute, Güero. I am working here. This is
my picture, un poco bigotón, pero is my picture."
"Güeno sí pero tú estás tomando tequila. Mucho
picoso."
"Nomás el primero pica, después se pica uno solo.
Échate un trago."
"Oh, no otra vez será!"
"Güeno, I wai[t] for you or you wai[t] for me.
¡Mejor you wai[t]!"

CANTADO   Yo les digo a mis amigos
los que vayan a las pizcas
no se dejen engañar.
Con los güeros ganen lana
pero no la han de gastar
vénganse pá la frontera
¡dónde si van a gozar!

Beautiful Borders

SPOKEN   Beautiful Northern Borders. How I miss you! I
haven't seen you in a year.

SUNG   I was traveling
Around the border cities.

Oh, what a beautiful sight!
From Tijuana to Juárez,
From Juárez to Laredo,
Then from Laredo to Matamoros
Without forgetting Reynosa.

SPOKEN   I remember the first time I went to the United States
of America. "I did not go on a pleasure trip there,
I went to pick cotton!" I wrote my mother a letter
telling her, "Mom, I have a new 'saco.' "[1] And
my mother went around the town making a big
fuss telling everybody, "My son is well-dressed.
He has a new 'saco'!" Heck, a new cotton-
picking sack!

SUNG   A young lady at the bridge,
Beautiful spring flower she was,
Kept looking and looking at me.
I asked her to please tell me
If she liked me.
But all she wanted was for me
To help her cross the bridge.

SPOKEN   She saw my strong arms, my wide shoulders. She
made me carry her stuff. Upon reaching the
customs office, the officer with the cap asked me,
"What have you, there?"
"Only whisky."
"Yeah, but you have a hundred cases!"
"Well, I am on a drinking spree and I don't drink
by the bottle, I drink by the case! Why don't you
take two of them?" And he did not take two. He
took them all!

SUNG   I used to go to the U.S.A.
Hiding from people,
For I was a wetback.
Now with my passport
I am within the law.
I drink my whisky or tequila
Even in the middle of the road.

SPOKEN   At that point the sheriff arrived, a big fellow about
two meters taller than I. We came face to face, in

[1] Play on words. *Saco* can mean coat or cotton-picking sack.

a matter of speaking. He was so tall I could only see his belt buckle.

"Hey, you Mexican. Are you a wetback?"

"Wait a minute, blondie. I am working here. This is my picture. My moustache is big but this is my picture."

"Well, yes, but you are drinking tequila. It is very hot."

"Only the first gulp, after that one cannot stop. Here, have a drink."

"Oh, no, another time!"

"Well, I will wait for you. Or you wait for me. Better yet, you wai[t]!"[2]

SUNG
    I tell my friends
    That when they go pick cotton
    Not to be deceived.
    To earn their money there
    But to spend it here on the border
    Where they can really have fun.

By the 1970s, the "illegal alien problem" had received a tremendous amount of publicity. Whether there has been an actual rise in undocumented workers crossing the United States or whether the post-Vietnam War depression and recession with their high level of unemployment have focused undue emphasis on the Mexican worker is open to question. Publicity and constant reports regarding increase in the number of "illegal aliens," however, have resulted in a number of folk songs with the *mojado* or wetback theme being written in this decade.

The next three songs are included in the "Proud-to-be-Mexican" category because of the general theme of optimism and self-confidence found in them.

"Cruzando el puente" (by R. Hernandez, recorded by Los Cadetes de Linares, in *Cruzando el Puente,* Ramex LP 1014, side 1) depicts a nostalgic bracero happy to be "crossing the bridge" back to Mexico. He brings with him fond memories of the United States. With an aching heart he bids farewell, acknowledging the beauty found in the United States, the "skyscrapers, its art, airports" and, of course, its beautiful women.

[2]Play on words: "*wai*" = *guey* or *buey,* 'ox' or 'stupid person' and/or cuckold.

Cruzando el puente

Ya parece que voy cruzando el puente
de Matamoros con rumbo a Valle Hermoso,
se divisan las praderas, y mis ríos
y los cantares de los pájaros hermosos.

Adiós Estados Unidos, me despido
de tus bellezas y tus artes tan preciosos,
tus edificios, aeropuertos y otras cosas,
y tus mujeres son las rosas más hermosas.

Adiós, adiós, adiós, adiós.
Yo ya me voy pa' no volver.
Lo que más quise se quedó
por no saberme comprender.

Adiós Estados Unidos, me despido, etc.

Crossing the Bridge

I feel like I am crossing the bridge
At Matamoros on my way to Valle Hermoso.
I can see the meadows, the river,
And hear the singing of the beautiful birds.

Good-bye United States, I say good-bye,
To your beauty and your precious art,
Your skyscrapers, your airports and other things,
And your women are the most beautiful roses.

Good-bye, good-bye, good-bye, good-bye.
I am leaving, I will not be back.
That which was dearest to me I leave behind,
Because she did not understand me.

Good-bye United States, I say good-bye, etc.

The song "Los alambrados" (by Marco Antonio Solís, recorded by Los Bukis in *Los alambrados,* Mericana Records MM 6625, side 1) derives its title (The Wire Jumpers) from the fact that those crossing illegally from Mexico to Southern California do not have a river to cross at the border and thus are not "wetbacks." Rather, they often have to climb or cut a wire fence. The term is applied to anybody crossing the border illegally into Southern California.

"Los alambrados" is a song about a group of men crossing the border through the Tijuana area, and it describes the experience of hiding in the bushes to escape the vigilant eye of the border patrol which searches the area with helicopters. The men make their way to Encinitas, California, and from there, with hope and strong faith, go on to Chicago. The song ends on a happy note stating that in Chicago they are earning dollars and spending them happily.

Los alambrados

HABLADO   "Ahora sí muchachos, a ganar muchos dólares."

CANTADO   De México habían salido
hasta Tijuana llegaron.
Por no tener sus papeles
de alambristas se pasaron.

Se cruzaron por el cerro.
Su rumbo habían agarrado,
iban rodeando veredas
como lo habían acordado
era de noche y por eso
la vigilancia burlaron.

Ya por allá en Chula Vista
dos tipos los esperaron
un helicóptero andaba
queriéndolos encontrar
pero entre los matorrales
nada pudieron mirar.
Lo que hay que hacer en la vida
para dólares ganar.

HABLADO   "¡Apúrale Leno!"
"¡Ora!"

CANTADO   Hasta Encinitas llegaron
casi ya de madrugada
de los que los recojieron
no se volvió a saber nada
allí pasaron dos noches
y sin poder hacer nada.

Más tarde se decidieron
a dar la vida o la muerte
la fe que tenían

los llevó con mucha suerte.
Ahora ya andan en Chicago,
con dólares se divierten.

The Wire Jumpers

SPOKEN   ''Now boys, we are going to earn a lot of dollars!''

SUNG   From Mexico City they came,
Arriving in Tijuana.
Because they did not have a passport,
As wire jumpers they crossed the border.

They went through the hills.
They followed the way
Close to the sideroads
As they had planned.
It was night
And that is why
The border patrol they fooled.

Around Chula Vista
Two men waited for them.
A helicopter was circling
Trying to apprehend them,
But hidden in the bushes
They were able to survive.
This is what a man must do
To earn his keep.

SPOKEN   ''Get with it, Leno!''
''Sure!''

SUNG   They arrived at Encinitas
Around the early dawn.
The men who took them
Disappeared without a trace.
There, they spent two nights
Without being able to move.

Later they decided
To risk life itself

Their strong faith in themselves
Brought them good luck.
Now they are in Chicago
Having fun with the dollars they earn.

"El corrido de los mojados" (Armenta, n.d.:23) is a currently popular corrido repeatedly being played on the local Spanish-speaking radio stations of Los Angeles.

The corrido starts by stating the hardships of the wetback, that is, avoiding the law all the time and being unable to speak English. They acknowledge the fact that there are thousands of men crossing the border repeatedly through all the major cities along the 2,000-mile boundary between the United States and Mexico. The "wetbacks," therefore, suggest a "simple" solution to their problem: find an Anglo woman, "gringuita," to marry and they will be illegals no more. This, of course, is said with tongue-in-cheek humor.

In a more serious vein, they realize and state their contribution to the United States economy and particularly the important role they play in the agricultural fields.

El corrido de los mojados

Porque somos los mojados
siempre nos busca la ley,
porque estamos ilegales
y no hablamos el inglés;
el gringo terco a sacarnos
y nosotros a volver.

Si uno(s) sacan por Laredo
por Mexicali entran diez,
si otro sacan por Tijuana
por Nogales entran seis;
ai nomás saquen la cuenta,
cuantos entramos al mes.

El problema de nosotros
fácil se puede arreglar:
que nos den una gringuita
para podernos casar;
y ya que nos de la mica
que se vuelva a divorciar.

Cuando el mojado haga huelga
a no volver otra vez,
quién va a tapar la cebolla,
lechuga y el vetabel;
el limón y la toronja,
se echará todo a perder.

Esos salones de baile
todos los van a cerrar,
porque si se va el mojado
quienes van ir a bailar;
y a más de cuatro gringuitas,
no las podrán consolar.

Vivan todos los mojados,
los que ya van a emigrar,
los que van de vacaciones
los que vienen a pasar;
y los que van a casarse
para poder arreglar.

The Corrido of the Wetbacks

Because we are wetbacks
The law is always after us,
Because of our illegal status
And cannot speak English;
The stubborn "gringo" chases us out
And with the same stubbornness we return.

If they kick one [wetback] out through Laredo
Ten will come in through Mexicali,
If another is kicked out through Tijuana
Six will come in through Nogales;
You just figure it out,
How many come in each month.

Our problem
Can easily be solved:
All we need is a "gringuita"
So that we can get married;
And after we get our green card [legal documents]
We can get a divorce.

When the wetback decides
Not to ever return [to the U.S.A.],
Who is going to take care of the onion fields,
The lettuce and the beets;
The lemon and the grapefruit?
All will rot in their place.

And the dancing halls
All will close their doors,
Because if the wetback leaves
Who is going to go dancing;
And more than four "gringuitas,"
Will be inconsolable.

Long live all the wetbacks,
[Long live] those that are ready to emigrate,
[Long live] those that vacation there
[Long live] those that are just passing by;
[Long live] those that go there to get married
So they can legally stay.

The Bracero Experience Satirized

The three songs that follow, written in the 1960s and 1970s, treat the bracero experience in a humorous, satirical manner. They deal more with the acculturation of the bracero than with his mistreatment. They are in the tradition of other comical United States–Mexican border type folk songs such as "Los Mexicanos que hablan inglés," an old folk song collected by Américo Paredes. The first two of these songs are sung by the extremely popular "El Piporro," a singer known for his songs about the lower classes living along the United States–Mexican border (La Frontera).

The song "Natalio Reyes Colás" (written and recorded by Eulalio González in *Lo mejor del Piporro,* Discos Musart DC 787, side 6) describes the partial transformation of a bracero. Natalio Reyes Colás is a lower class "dude" (*pelao*) who decides to cross the Río Grande leaving his girl friend behind. Upon entering the United States, he finds a Chicana who transforms his name to Nat King Cole. Soon "Nat" forgets about his girl back home, forgets his songs, and his food. He has become an assimilated Mexican who likes rock and roll. Mabel, the Chicana he met, disappoints him because she cannot cook tortillas. She can only cook American food such as waffles, hamburgers, and ham and eggs. So Natalio Reyes Colás, alias Nat King Cole, decides to return to his beloved "Petrita," his girl friend in Mexico.

Natalio Reyes Colás

HABLADO   Ya no vuelvo al otro "lao" porque no sé hablar
inglés, y los que lo saben, pos no me entienden.

CANTADO   Natalio Reyes Colás
de Tamaulipas nacido,
pelado fino y audaz
el río Bravo crecido
cruzó sin mirar pa' trás,
dejando novia, comprometido,
con quien casar.

No era flaca, era gordita,
Petra Garza Benavides
Reyes Colás no me olvides,
soy más bien feya que hermosa
pero no te hayas otra
que sea más hacendosa.

HABLADO   Nomás cruzó la línea divisoria por el otro "lao" y se
encontró con Mabel, Mabel Ortiz, una pochita que
hasta el nombre le cambió, en vez de Natalio, le
puso Nat, en vez de Reyes, King, y Cole por
Colás. Ahora es Nat King Cole Martínez de la
Garza.

CANTADO   Bracero, bracero, ya no quiere polka
con el acordeón, ora se enoja
al compás del rock and roll.
Olvidó a Petrita, quiere a la pochita
y hasta le canta como Nat King Cole.

HABLADO   Pero la pochita lo dejó en la calle no sabía más que
cantar y bailar, de cocinar nada, puro ham and
eggs, waffles and jambarger con cachup y aquel
estaba impuesto a pura tortilla con chile.

CANTADO   Natalio Reyes Colás
se regresó a la frontera,
se vino a pata y en "ride"
diciendo yo no he de hallar
otra prietita que me quiera
como Petrita, aunque feyita
si sabe amar.

Natalio Reyes Colás

SPOKEN
I am not going back to the U.S.A. Because I do not
speak English, and those that can speak it do not
understand me.

SUNG
Natalio Reyes Colás,
Native of Tamaulipas,
A bold and fine "dude,"
Crossed the Río Bravo.
He crossed it without looking back,
Leaving his fiancee,
Whom he had planned to marry.

She wasn't skinny, she was chubby
Petra Garza Benavides.
Crying, she told Natalio:
"Reyes Colás, do not forget me.
I am on the ugly side, I know,
But this I can tell you.
You will not find a
Better housekeeper than me."

SPOKEN
As soon as he crossed the line, he found another girl,
Mabel, Mabel Ortiz, a Chicana, who even
changed his name. Instead of Natalio, she named
him Nat, and instead of Reyes, King, and for
Colás, Cole. Now he is Nat King Cole Martínez
de la Garza.

SUNG
Bracero, bracero, he does not like polkas,
With the accordions, now he goes wild
With the rhythm of rock and roll.
He forgot Petrita, he likes the little Chicana:
And he even sings to her like Nat King Cole.

SPOKEN
But the little Chicana left him on the streets. She only
knew how to sing and dance. She couldn't cook,
only ham and eggs, Waffles, and hamburgers with
ketchup, And the "dude" was used to tortillas and
hot peppers.

SUNG
Natalio Reyes Colás
Returned to the Mexican border.
He walked and asked for a ride
Saying I shall never find
A dark-skinned girl

Like little Petra; even though she's ugly
She knows how to love.

"Juan Mojao" (written and recorded by Eulalio González in *A lo Piporro*, Discos Musart TEDM 10656, side 1), or John Wetback, is the second of the songs sung by "El Piporro." This time the name of the main character changes from Juan Pancho to Johnny Frankie. Again, Juan Pancho is a poor peasant, who, upon entering the United States, gives up his corridos for rock and roll and becomes a stylish "dude" with high platform shoes and stacked heels. The "huarachis" or sandals of his humble Mexican origins have been forgotten.

But as luck would have it, the border patrol catches up with him and he is forced to walk back to the border. As his tired feet become more and more irritated from the long trek, he wishes he had his "huarachis."

Juan Mojao

CANTADO   Al cruzar el Río Grande
             al entrar en U.S.A.
             se olvidó hasta de su nombre
             no Juan Pancho, no more Pancho
             Johnny Frankie if its O.K.

             Ya no canta más corridos
             pa' las güeras lus en rol
             pantalón de abajo ancho
             plataforma y gran tacón
             chus de onda
             nice zapatos
             no huarachis anymore, anymore.

HABLADO   Y de repente que se oye el grito—¡Ay viene la migra!
             Por papeles "traiba" mica falsa que un malvado le
                 vendió y a pies hasta South of the Border la
                 migración lo llevó.

             Y me fui de mojao y a pura lumbre me sentaron.

CANTADO   El monte agarró Juan Pancho
             evitando las veredas
             pa' no dejar que sus huellas
             le hicieran ellas volver sus pasos
             pa' donde ya no quería estar.

Llevaba Pancho entre ceja y ceja
Frontera Norte poder cruzar.
Su pobre jacal dejaba
y en cuanto más se alejaba
pos menos quería mirarlo
no fuera a ser que el jacal
le viera sus intenciones de no volver
tampoco quiso que se supiera
que iba llorando sin contener.

Se acabaron chus de onda
ni siquiera sus huarachis
para alivio de sus pies
sus pobres pies que quemaron una y otra y otra vez.

El monte agarró Juan Pancho
evitando las veredas
pa' no dejar que sus huellas
le hicieran ellas volver sus pasos
a donde ya no quería estar.
Llevaba Pancho entre ceja y ceja
Frontera Norte poder cruzar.

John Wetback

SUNG

Upon crossing the Rio Grande,
Upon entering the U.S.A.,
He forgot even his name.
Not Juan Pancho, no more Pancho,
Johnny Frankie, if its O.K.

He doesn't sing corridos
For the blondies, rock and roll,
Bell-bottom pants,
Platform shoes, stacked heels,
Stylish shoes,
Great shoes,
Not huarachis anymore, anymore.

SPOKEN

And suddenly one hears the shout: "Here come the immigration officers!" His documents are a false border-crossing card that an evil man sold him.

And he was forced to walk all the way to South
of the Border by the immigration officers.

I went as a wetback and got grilled by the police.

SUNG   Juan Pancho took the back trails
            So that his footsteps could not
            Force him to return to the place
            He did not want to be.

            Pancho had in his mind
            To cross the border back into the U.S.A.
            He again left his hut.
            And as he went farther and farther away
            He did not want to look back.
            He was afraid his little hut
            Could read his plans
            Of never coming back.
            He did not want anyone to know
            That he was crying profusely.

            His stylish shoes are gone.
            Not even his sandals
            Did he have for the relief
            Of his tired feet.
            His poor tired feet that burned
            Over and over again.

            Juan Pancho took the back trails
            So that his footprints could not
            Force him to return to the
            Place he did not want to be.
            Juan Pancho had in mind
            To cross the border into the U.S.A.

The third song dealing with the theme of acculturation is "Uno
más de los mojados" (written by José Manuel Figueroa, recorded
by Antonio Aguilar in *La muerte de un gallero*, Discos Musart ED-
1721, side B). Here the story is told about a man named Pancracio
who emigrates to the United States illegally from the Ranch of the
Grunt in Mexico. He swims across the river bringing with him his
sole pair of pants with holes in them. Soon Pancracio is making
good in the United States; he even appears on television—evi-
dently he is a janitor at a television station.

Pancracio writes home about his difficulty with the English
language and how he is beginning to forget Spanish to which his

buddies wisely reply, "You had better return before you forget how to speak!"

Pancracio, however, meets and falls in love with doña María and soon they are "sharing a mattress." Pancracio is humorously depicted as a Don Juan flirting with blond Anglo girls who do not pay attention to him until he starts earning good money. Too late, Pancracio is no longer interested. He is happily working on the railroad tracks in Arkansas.

Uno más de los mojados

HABLADO	¡Ay mis cuates! Esta canción se llama "Uno más de los mojaos" dedicado a tanto pelao que han entrado ilegalmente a United States. ¡Ay te va pa' mi compadre Pancracio. ¡Ay te voy compadre!
CANTADO	Cuando Pancracio vino a este país de güeros solamente agujeros el traía en el pantalón.
	No se sorprendan que esta es la verdad y alcabo se coló por el Río Bravo y escapó del azadón.
	Era Pancracio uno más de los mojados que traían siempre asoliados a la heroica migración.
	Y ahora Pancracio con los años que ha pasado me dirán si no ha progresado mírenlo en televisión.
HABLADO	¡Limpia los baños! ¡Limpia los baños!
CANTADO	"Good morning prieta," le decía a cualquier güereja que encontraba en la banqueta y ella no le hacía jalón.
	Y ahora las gordas como estamos en carencia andan buscando su herencia y él les dice, "Leave me alone!"
HABLADO	Sí porque el viejo aprendió inglés. Si amigo. Saben que Pancracio se fue a los United States y a los seis meses les escribió a todos sus cuates acá en el rancho del Pujido y les decía, "Olvídaseme el español y dificúltaseme el inglés." Y sus cuates le dicen: "Pos regrésate güey ¡antes que te quedes mudo!"
CANTADO	Pero un güen día se encontró a Doña María, le juró que la amaría y le entregó su corazón.

Y así pusieron un puestote de cacahuates
compartieron el petate y comparten el colchón.

HABLADO   ¿No que te ha ido tan bien?

CANTADO   "Good morning, prieta," le decía a cualquier güereja
que encontraba en la banqueta y ella no le hacía
jalón.

Y ahora las gordas como estamos en carencia
andan buscando su herencia y él les dice, "Leave me
alone!"

HABLADO   Como el pelao está trabajando en el traque allá en
"Arkenso" [Arkansas]. Allá en "Arkenso" allá
anda el viejo. ¡Allá les voy!

CANTADO   "Good morning, prieta," le decía a cualquier güereja
que encontraba en la banqueta y ellas no le hacían
jalón.

Y ahora las gordas como estamos ya en carencia
andan buscando su herencia y él les dice, "Leave me
alone!"

HABLADO   Que quiere decir: ¡Déjenme en paz! ¡Déjenme en
paz! "Go away, güey!"

One More Wetback

SPOKEN   Oh, my "brothers!" This song is called "One More
Wetback." It is dedicated to all those dudes who
have entered the United States illegally. Here goes!
For my compadre Pancracio! Here I go compadre!

SUNG   When Pancracio came to this country of blondes
The only thing he carried in his pants were holes.

Don't be surprised. This is the truth and anyway
He crossed the Rio Bravo and escaped the hoe.

Pancracio was one of these wetbacks
Who always had those heroic immigration officers
jumping.

Now Pancracio with the passing years

Has progressed quite a bit; you can see him at the
T.V. station.

SPOKEN   He cleans bathrooms! He cleans bathrooms!

SUNG   "Good morning, honey," he would tell any blonde
He saw on the street and she would ignore him.

But now that we are in a recession
They are looking for money
And he tells them, "Leave me alone!"

SPOKEN   Yes, you see, the old man learned English. Yes, my
friend. You see, Pancracio went to the United
States and after six months he wrote back home to
all his buddies here at the Ranch of the Grunt.
He wrote: "I am forgetting Spanish and English is
getting more difficult." And his buddies replied:
"Well, you had better return before you forget
how to speak, you ox!"

SUNG   But one fine day, he met María.
He swore he loved her and gave her his heart.

And that is how they set up a peanut stand.
They shared a straw mat and now share a mattress.

SPOKEN   Aren't you well off?

SUNG   "Good morning, honey," he would tell any blonde
He saw on the street and she would ignore him.

But now that we are in a recession
They are looking for money
And he tells them, "Leave me alone!"

SPOKEN   You see, the "dude" is working on the railroad
tracks over there in Arkansas. There in Arkansas
the old man is! Here I go!

SUNG   "Good morning, honey," he would tell any blondie
He would see on the street and she would ignore him.

But now that we are in a recession
They are looking for money and he tells them,
"Leave me alone!"

SPOKEN   Which means: "Leave me in peace, leave me in
peace. Get lost, creep!"

The Homesick Bracero

The two folk songs that follow deal primarily with the nostalgic theme of being away from one's country and one's family.

"Paso del Norte" is a traditional folk song that has retained its popularity owing in part to its theme of homesickness. The name of the folk song is derived from the geographical term applied to the Juárez-El Paso border-crossing area. The bracero sings of the loneliness he feels as he leaves the area behind. He fondly recalls his parents, his brothers, his girl, and moanfully sings about his pain of parting from them.

Paso del Norte

Qué triste se encuentra el hombre
cuando anda ausente
cuando anda ausente
allá lejos de su patria

Piormente si se acuerda
de sus padres y su chata
¡Ay que destino!
Para sentarme a llorar.

Paso del Norte
que lejos te vas quedando
sus divisiones
de mi se están alejando

Los pobres de mis hermanos
de mi se están acordando
¡Ay que destino!
Para sentarme a llorar.

Paso del Norte
que lejos te vas quedando.
Tus divisiones
de mi se están alejando

Los pobres de mis hermanos
de mi se están acordando
¡Ay que destino!
para sentarme a llorar.

The Northern Pass

How sad man becomes
When he is far away
When he is far away
From his own country.

It is worse when he remembers
his parents and his girl.
What a cruel destiny!
One could sit down and cry!

Oh, Northern Pass!
How far I am leaving you!
Your boundary lines
are getting farther and farther away!

My poor brothers
are all thinking about me.
What a cruel destiny!
One could sit down and cry!

Oh, Northern Pass!
How far I am leaving you!
Your boundary lines
are getting farther and farther away.

My poor brothers
are all thinking about me.
What a cruel destiny!
One could sit down and cry!

The song "Lamento de un bracero" (written by Paco Camacho, recorded by Antonio Aguilar in *Soy inocente*, Discos Musart EDM 1700, side 3) depicts a sick bracero suffering mentally and physically his imprisonment in an American jail. For an unexplained reason he finds himself a prisoner somewhere in the United States. The bracero expresses his chagrin through the lyrics of this song and laments his present condition, his feelings of helplessness, of loneliness, of finding himself so far away from friends, relatives, and country. He is indeed a homesick bracero!

Lamento de un bracero

CANTADO   Dentro de una celda oscura
está llorando un bracero

es un ranchero valiente
que lo hicieron prisionero.

Sentado frente a la reja
soportando el frío invierno
él ya se siente morir
pues se encuentra muy enfermo.

Se oye que dice el bracero
—¡O virgencita morena
no quiero morir aquí
quiero morir en mi tierra!

HABLADO   ¡Ay mis amigos, cuídense de esa canija *migrechón!*

CANTADO   Se acerca a la ventanilla
y contempla las estrellas
se acuerda de sus amigos
de su familia y su tierra.

Se oye que dice el bracero
—¡O virgencita morena
no quiero morir aquí
quiero morir en mi tierra!

Bracero's Lament

SUNG   Inside a dark cell
Lies a bracero crying.
He is a brave rancher
Who was taken prisoner.

Seated in front of the cell bars,
Feeling the bitter cold,
He is near dying,
He is gravely ill.

One can hear the bracero saying:
"Oh, my dark virgin!
I do not want to die here.
I want to die in my land."

SPOKEN   My friends, be careful of those sneaky immigration
officers.

SUNG   He walks toward the window
            And stares at the stars.
            He remembers his friends
            His family and his land.

            One can hear the bracero saying:
            "Oh my dark virgin!
            I do not want to die here.
            I want to die in my land."

Bracero Protest Songs

The protest song is a cry against social injustice suffered by the Mexican worker in the United States. It describes the low pay for the hard work performed, the humiliation, the inhumane treatment, and other inequities the bracero undergoes on the farms of the United States.

The oldest of the three corridos, "Corrido de los desarraigados" (Cardozo-Freeman, 1976:132), was written by the New Mexican folk-poet Arnulfo Castillo in 1942.

Inez Cardozo-Freeman has analyzed Castillo's work in the following manner (Cardozo-Freeman, 1976:132–133):

He [Castillo] is no longer living in Mexico but in the United States and under circumstances which cause him great pain, great humiliation and unhappiness. He crossed the river to become a bracero, as did millions like him on a contractual basis with the United States during WW II.

He feels strongly that he has lost something of great value to him, that is, his honor and his homeland. Now he is in exile, an alien from his beloved Mexico. Life in Mexico had always been difficult; it had always been full of hard labor and pain, but in spite of this there had been joy, joy in one's sense of self, joy in nature and the freedom of the country-side, joy in his manhood, and above all, his honor. In this *corrido,* however, all the joyful part of life has been taken away. Only the insult to honor and the misery of hard work and low pay remain. And worse, there is the feeling of being thought of as inferior, as one who is to be used. He is one of the uprooted ones; he does not belong, he is not welcome. He is a man without honor or country in a strange and inhospitable land. It is a bitter song. In it he sings not only of his loss but laments at the foolishness of himself and others like him who deserted Mexico to serve a new homeland that does not welcome them as fellow human beings but, rather, welcomes only their capacity for hard and cheap labor. He also complains that his fellow countrymen, as soon as they cross the border, deny their motherland. He believes that being so willing to desert one's homeland is in itself a dishonorable act. This *corrido* is one more in a long tradition of protest *corridos*. It is a protest against the injustices suffered by the Mexican *braceros* in the United States.

Corrido de los desarraigados

Señores, pongan cuidado / lo que es verdad yo les digo.
Como México no hay dos / por lindo, hermoso y florido.

Toditos los extranjeros / lo tienen pa' su delirio.
Del cuarenta y tres atrás / no se hallaba complicado.

México, México era muy feliz / sincero, humilde y honrado
Hasta que empezó a cruzar / la raza pa'l otro lado.

Contratistas y troqueros / pa' mi todos son iguales,
No más 'taban esperando / que pasaran nacionales.

Parecían lobos hambrientos / fuera de los matorrales.
Los creemos con honor / pero no lo(s) conocemos.

Nos trabajan como esclavos / y nos tratan como perros,
No más falta que nos monten / y que nos pongan el freno.

Si alguno lo toma a mal / es que no lo ha conocido
Que se vaya a contratar / a los Estados Unidos.

Y verá que va trabajar / como un esclavo vendido.
Antes éramos honrados / y de eso nada ha quedado.

Con eso del pasaporte / nos creemos americanos
Pero tenemos el nombre / de ser desarraigados.

Allí les va la despedida / a toditos mis paisanos
Si quieren tener honor / no vayan al otro lado
A mantener contratistas / y los troqueros hambrientos.

The Corrido of the Uprooted Ones

Men, pay attention / What I say is true.
There is no other country like Mexico / beautiful, lush green.

All the foreigners / are amazed by Mexico.
Previous to 1943 / there were no complications.

Mexico, Mexico was happy / sincere, humble, honest
Until our race started crossing / to the other side.

Contractors and truckers / to me they are all the same,
They were only waiting / for nationals to cross.

They resembled hungry wolves / outside their thicket.
We believe they are honorable / but we don't know them.

They work us like slaves / and treat us like dogs.
All we need is for them to ride us / and to put the bridle on us.

If someone doesn't like what I say / its because he wasn't there.
Let him go as a bracero / to the United States.

He will see that he will work / like a sold slave.
Before we were honorable men / now we have lost it all.

With our passports / we think we are Americans.
But we are called / the uprooted ones.

Here I bid farewell / to all my countrymen.
If you want to have honor / don't go to the other side
To feed the contractors / and hungry truckers.

"El corrido del ilegal," written in the 1970s by Francisco García (recorded by Francisco García and Pablo and Juanita Saludado in *Las voces de los campesinos*, FM SC-1, side 1), protests the exploitation of undocumented workers who have left Mexico because of hunger. The lyrics of the corrido depict the close working relationship between immigration officers, farmers, and contractors who work together to the detriment of the worker. The illegal alien finds himself being used as a strike breaker, a scab. This corrido is a strong statement against such conspiratorial maneuvering, especially the ever present evil incarnate "contratista" or contractor. A note of humor is introduced in the last verse when the illegal aliens are bitten by wasps!

El corrido del ilegal

Andando yo en la frontera
Ya me cargaba el hambre.
Dicen que el hambre es canija,
Pero es más del que ya le ande.
Me pasé al otro lado.
Tuve que hacerla de alambre.

A los poquitos momentos
Me agarra la inmigración.
Me dice, "Tú eres alambre."
Le contesté, "Sí, señor."
"De eso no tengas cuidado
Tal vez tengas tú razón."

"Si tú quieres trabajar
Nomás que no seas Chavista,
Yo mismo te he de llevar
A manos del contratista.
Le estamos dando la chanza
A todos los alambristas."

Nos llevaron para un campo
Juntos con chavos de escuela.
Rodeados de policía
Que provocaban la guerra
Para quebrar una huelga
En el valle de Coachella.

Policías e inmigración
Unidos con los rancheros,
Conspiración contratista
Por el maldito dinero.
En contra de nuestra gente
Parecían unos perros.

Dormíamos bajo las viñas,
Todo el bonche de alambristas.
Y para el peor de la ruina
Nos picaron las avispas
No nos dio ni medicina,
El desgraciado contratista.

Después salimos en huelga
Para ayudar a la unión.
El desgraciado contratista
Nos echó la inmigración.
Esposados de las manos
Nos llevan a la prisión.

Yo les digo a mis amigos.
"Más vale jalar parejo;
Nunca cruzen la frontera

En calidad de conejo,
Menos a quebrar La Huelga.
Que ya no sean tan pendejos.''

The Corrido of the Illegal Worker

As I was walking along the border
I was already burdened by hunger.
They say that hunger is unrelenting,
But it is more than that to the one who suffers from it.
I crossed over to the other side.
I had to make it under the wire.

In a few moments
The Immigration caught me.
He said to me, ''You are illegal.''
I answered, ''Yes, sir.''
''Don't worry about it,
Perhaps you are right.''

''If you want to work,
As long as you're not a Chavista,
I myself will take you
To a contractor.
We are giving an opportunity
To all the wire jumpers.''

They took us to a field
Together with school kids.
We were surrounded by policemen
Who provoked a fight
In order to break the strike
In the Coachella Valley.

Police and Immigration
Together with the growers,
This was the contractors' conspiracy
For the sake of evil money.
Against our people
They acted like dogs.

We slept under the vines,
The whole bunch of wire jumpers.

And to top it all off
The wasps stung us.
That wretched contractor
Did not even give us medicine.

Later we went on strike
In order to help the union.
The wretched contractor
Turned the Immigration on us.
They took us handcuffed
To prison.

I tell my friends,
"It is better not to scab;
Never cross the border
Like a rabbit,
Let alone to break The Strike.
Don't be so stupid anymore."

"La descriminación" (written by Juan Manuel and Leobardo
Pérez, recorded by Dueto América in *De México a Laredo,* Caliente
CLT 7242, side 2), as the title suggests, complains of the discriminatory treatment given to the Mexican illegal. This song, like
some of the fictional works analyzed, places the blame on the
bracero himself. In the first verse we are told that the bracero is
coming to the United States because of greed and an adventurous
spirit.

The bracero finds in the United States hard work and ill-treatment because he is a foreigner. He finally is turned in by an
"envious" neighbor. Upon his arrival in Mexico, he finds his
mother gravely ill and dying, the implication being that he is
receiving punishment from God for leaving his country. In desperation, the bracero promises one of the Catholic saints, Santo Niño,
that if his mother gets well he will never leave her side again.

La descriminación

Dejé mi patria por mi afán aventurero
Y a California me marché sin dilación.
Por la ilusión calenturienta del dinero
partí en pedazos de mi madre el corazón.

Y lavaplatos, ayudante y cocinero
sin hacer caso de la descriminación

en el trabajo por mi origen extranjero
se iba empiorando cada día la situación.

En una noche que a mi casa regresaba
frente a una iglesia me aprendió la inmigración
me denunciaron por envidia mis vecinos
y me mandaron de regreso a mi nación.

> Solo un consejo yo les doy a mis hermanos
> A los que se hallan de aventura por allá
> que se regresen que en su patria los esperan
> sus familiares y también su libertad.

Cuando a mi rancho nuevamente regresaba
con intenciones de ponerme a descansar
mi madre enferma agonizante me esperaba
era tan triste el panorama de mi hogar.

Al Santo Niño le rogué que la curara
y hasta juré que no la vuelvo a bandonar.

> Solo un consejo yo les doy a mis hermanos
> etc.

Discrimination

I left my country because of my adventurous spirit,
To California I went without delay.
With the burning illusion of making money,
I broke in a thousand pieces my mother's heart.

And as a dishwasher, helper, and cook,
Without heeding the discriminatory treatment
I got at work for being a foreigner,
Each day the situation became worse.

One night when I was returning home
In front of a church the immigration officers caught me.
My envious neighbors had turned me in
And I was returned to my country.

> I have but one word of advice for my friends,
> The ones that are still over there.
> To return, for here in your country,
> Your family waits for you and your liberty too.

When I returned to my ranch
With the intent of resting,
My sick dying mother waited for me.
It was a sad picture I found indeed.

I begged the Santo Niño to cure her.
I even promised I would never leave her.

I have but one word of advice, etc.

Two of the protest corridos, "El corrido del ilegal" and "El corrido de los desarraigados," were written by Mexicans living in the United States. This important fact sets these protest songs apart from the general corpus of songs with bracero content. The Chicano and the Mexican who have lived in the United States are generally more politicized. During the Civil Rights movement of the 1960s and early 1970s, Chicanos became more politically aware and militantly verbal about the differences in economic, social, and political status between themselves and the Anglo majority.

Too, Cesar Chavez's organizing activities drew attention to problems that were present in the agricultural fields. The discrepancy in attitude between the protest corridos and the other corridos is attributable in large part to the fact that while the bracero was comparing his experience in the United States with the conditions he had left in Mexico, the Chicano is comparing his position or standard of living vis-à-vis that of the Anglo population.

Comment on the Folk Song

Comparison of lore about the bracero experience in the folk songs and in Pedro's story shows similarity in attitudes not much evident in fiction. The songs, particularly the satirical, ironic ones, reflect a picaresque being generally imbued with a wit, intelligence, and extraordinary ability for survival. This aspect of the bracero personality is not generally evident in the fictional works analyzed, except for Topete's *The Adventures of a Bracero.*

It is therefore clear that the folk song is more closely attuned to the bracero's desires, philosophy, and goals than are the works of fiction examined. This is certainly not surprising since the folk song is a form of lyrical expression which the lower class bracero has adopted as his own. As representatives of those who come from this class, those who write corridos, then, more adequately express the sentiments of their people than do the authors of the novels and short stories who are more educated and frequently come from the middle or upper classes of Mexican society.

Conclusion

In the final analysis there is an irreconcilable difference between the points of view held by the literary writers and those held by the braceros interviewed in Huecorio. The writers describe the bracero experience from an intellectual point of view, judging the peasant by their higher standards of comfort, wages, and education. The bracero sees his life in a completely different frame: as an impoverished individual having no job, no personal comforts, and living at a subsistence level, the bracero program and undocumented entry to the United States have represented for him the possibility of escape from his environment. In coming to the United States, for example, the bracero portrayed here in Pedro's story was able to obtain three good meals a day, have a steady job, and surround himself with comforts unknown at home in Mexico. To the bracero, then, this was a positive gain. To a middle class Mexican observer, of course, such gains were offset in fictional works by wretched foreign exploitation at the expense of the Mexican nation. As Richard Hancock (1959a:2) points out:

There has been much superficial discussion of this migration, almost all of it unfavorable. To the Mexican politicians and press this exodus is a "hemorrhage" of the nation's best blood; to most United States social, religious, and labor leaders, it is a large-scale exploitation of human misery by a few Southwestern corporation farmers. Most critics have a negative approach to this problem; they oppose continued migration but offer no realistic alternative. Many Mexican intellectuals feel duty-bound to berate supposed casual agents of this movement, but very few have made a serious study of the social and economic ramifications involved. These intellectuals, viewing the phenomenon as an embarrassing manifestation of the inadequacy of Mexican leadership, would like to see the migrant remain at home but offer no effective plan to give him an incentive to do so.

As portrayed by many novelists: the bracero comes back to Mexico a bitter, broken man—witness the characterizations in *Los que vuelven* by Juan Bustillo Oro, *Murieron a mitad del río* by Luis Spota, *Tenemos sed* by Magdalena Mondragón, *El dólar viene del norte* by J. de Jesús Becerra González, *Pobre patria mía* by María Luisa

121

Melo de Remes, and *Huelga blanca* by Héctor Raúl Almanza. The much more common experience of the bracero who is eager to come home to show off his acquisitions is rarely portrayed, as in *La región más transparente* by Carlos Fuentes; and it is the usual experience for the bracero to feel impatient to return to the United States after a brief stay in Mexico.

Investigators who corroborate Pedro's story include Hancock and George:

Despite the occasional abuses which Mexican workers suffer at the hands of United States farmers, one of the happiest aspects of the bracero program is the personal relationship that develops between workers and farmers. The mutual pleasure and cordiality with which workers and their employers greet each other when the worker arrives with a new contract after a long absence in Mexico are unmistakable. It is a rewarding experience to witness the departure of braceros at the end of the season, to see a Spanish-speaking farmer say farewell to a group of his homeward-bound braceros, embracing each one individually and calling him by his first name. The well-fed, well-dressed, happy men who, wearing their inevitable new Stetson hats, depart for Mexico carrying shiny new trunks and great, clanking canvas-wrapped bundles containing everything from plows to sewing machines, can hardly be recognized as the lean, ragged, worn-looking men that arrived in the United States in the spring with their possessions in small burlap bags.

The famed anthropologist Foster who has done much research on Mexican peasants coming from the Lake Patzcuaro area, of which Huecorio is a part, reports the following (1967:276):

Responsible braceros sent dollar checks to their families to support them during their absence, and to build up capital used to improve houses or buy land. Other braceros seemed to forget their families, and there were cases in which mother and children suffered because of this neglect. Still, on the whole, wives were pleased when their husbands went to the United States, because of the economic improvement it meant to them. Returning braceros brought from 100 to 300 dollars worth of presents to their families, in the form of clothing, transistor radios, and mechanical gadgets. Including the value of presents, checks sent home by mail, and cash brought at the end of the trip, a man lucky enough to work steadily for six months might clear from 10,000 to 15,000 pesos. Counting those whose contracts were much shorter, forty days was the legal minimum, average earnings were considerably less, perhaps in the 2,000 to 7,000 peso range.

Economic gain was the major factor in wanting to be bracero, but especially among the younger men, the opportunity to see the world was also an important motivation. In a rural society that lacks government and private scholarships for foreign travel and study, being a bracero was the only way open to young men to travel far from home and see how life is in another country. Consequently, the hardships and sometimes unfair treatment braceros experienced were usually looked upon as part of the game. If Tzintzuntzan is a fair sample, the accounts in the United States of bracero abuse and exploitation are greatly exaggerated. Of the scores of returned braceros with whom I have talked, not one has said he would not like to return.

The works of fiction analyzed do not present the complete picture and for political purposes often distort the reality described. Many of the Latin American writers examined took the point of view that art must serve a useful social purpose and neglected important literary aspects to the detriment of the work (see Eagleton 1976:46–47). Magdalena Mondragón, for example, in the introduction to her novel *Tenemos sed,* is lauded by the editors of *El Nacional,* sponsors of the literary contest which Mondragón won for her novel, with the following words:

. . . it is very satisfying for *El Nacional,* the daily newspaper serving Mexico, to publish Magdalena Mondragón's interesting and thought-provoking novel. Through her elegant pen she touches upon a parade of national problems focused from a superior angle: to love one's country through literature (p. 6).

Novelists such as Luis Spota stated the view commonly held by most Mexican intellectuals that bracero earnings were extremely low, in some cases so low that the braceros made absolutely no money. Spota wrote (1948:48) that the bracero

had come, he had suffered, for what? What had he gained? Not a thing except the desperation he carried within him. Why in heavens did all those Mexicans come to Texas? Where were those heaps of dollars that he envisioned when he embarked on this adventure? All he had left from all those months were the memories imprinted in his skin: scars that could map out his itinerary [in the United States].

All Mexican elites did not take such a position, however, and some have accepted the U.S. figure of $40 million annually sent home to Mexico (see Hancock 1967). As reported in the U.S. *Hearings on Mexican Labor* (1958:367): "Mexican Agricultural Minister Gilberto Flores Muñoz acknowledged in 1956 that braceros were the greatest dollar source after tourism and many stated that the bracero program did more than any other single thing to create a middle class of Mexican farmers." Pedro's story confirms that attitude in the braceros interviewed who all seemed to think their experience was worthwhile monetarily speaking.

In most of the fictional works discussed here, the authors seeking to drive home a sociological or political point present the bracero in a one-sided manner. Their fictional bracero, with some exceptions, are too bitter, lack the sense of humor, fortitude, and resilience that are the rich natural resources found in real-life braceros. In their zeal to present the bracero's experience as a shameful betrayal of government leaders of the Mexican Revolution's ideals, fiction writers neglected the bracero himself; they neglected to show the positive gains Mexico acquired as a result of having its citizenry abroad. No one can deny the beneficial aspects reaped as a result of traveling and coming in touch with a totally different culture. The bracero came home a new man—a man aware of his environment and his potential. Most of the braceros in Huecorio improved their standard of living. The money earned in the United States was used for home improvements, tool acquisitions including those for carpentry, sewing, masonry, hair-cutting implements and others. The most important single thing acquired, however, was not of a material nature but of an educational one and that is a willingness, a new disposition to accept change and to adopt new modes of life.

As most anthropologists have noted one of the most important elements in keeping a backward society from taking its place in a modern world is the inability or the resistance of the peasant society to change. Peasants are by nature conservative. As George M. Foster points out (1967:3): "Envious of the more fortunate peoples they see and hear about, they are nonetheless bound up in a cocoon of custom where the traditions and values of earlier generations still are seen as the safest guideposts to life." The breaking of these bonds with the past is one of the most difficult tasks confronting the government of a developing country. The peasant has strong emotional attachments to the past. To him what was adequate for his ancestors is suitable for him. That Huecorio has changed so much is in large part because of the bracero experience (see Belshaw 1967). So, too, has Tzintzuntzan changed, as Foster (1967:275) notes:

More important than urban migration, as an influence for change and economic improvements, has been the temporary migration of braceros to the United States, and especially to California and Texas. . . . By 1960 two hundred men—almost 50 percent of the adult males—had visited the United States at least once, and a number had returned year after year.

This exposure more than any other event seems to me to have changed the village. It is a mistake to assume that attitudes and views of every bracero are vastly modified by his American experience. Many return and take up their old ways with no apparent change whatsoever. But new attitudes and ideas are there.

A new awareness of other life-styles is therefore one of the primary contributions the bracero has brought to Mexico. As Gamio C. León has pointed out (1961:28):

> Some of the millions of Mexican braceros, or farm laborers, who have worked in the United States over the years have, on their return, stimulated social change in communities that seemed destined to be changeless.
>
> It is true that in various regions of the United States, they are the embittered victims of racial, cultural and economic discrimination, but on the other hand they improve themselves enormously without losing their essential character as Mexicans. In that new environment they are obliged, whether they want to or not, to change their material lives for the better. Their food includes meat, milk, bread, as well as tortillas when they can get them. They replace their sandals with shoes, and on holidays many of them wear wool suits. They have beds instead of mats to sleep in, plus furniture, no matter how simple, and in many cases running water, toilet, radio, and other conveniences. They go to the doctor and consume modern medicines. They learn to plant, cultivate, and harvest with modern techniques, and become familiar with various industries and the use of efficient tools and machinery. . . .
>
> The unexpected way that various sections of the Laguna region and of the lower Rio Grande Valley (Rio Brave) flourished because of the intensive activities of groups of repatriated braceros is a fine example.

This analysis fits the braceros I interviewed in Huecorio. They were the most forward-looking elements in that small community. It was very gratifying to learn that many bracero earnings coupled with bracero aspirations had made it possible for many of their younger brothers and sisters or if old enough their sons and daughters to acquire a profession. Many of the braceros interviewed were very proud to report that their bracero savings had made it possible for their kin to become engineers, teachers, and secretaries.

The braceros I interviewed in Huecorio did not come back with a revolutionary zeal to overthrow the present government of Mexico, but they did come back with a newly acquired political awareness and with previously unthought of criticisms directed at many of Mexico's traditionally corrupt aspects of life such as border inspection procedures by immigration officials. Even some of the priests could be criticized for engaging in securing bracero contracts, even if the forced "donation" did go to the church. Such criticism extended to banks, who make it almost impossible for farmers to secure proper loans, and to the ever present *coyotes*, agents who usually for an exorbitant amount promise to secure what is desired and who too often disappear with the funds.[1] The net effect of such criticism brought new sophistication to the bracero, who has begun to demand a more honest government.

Pedro's story shows the complexity of the bracero experience. If the main complaints of the braceros were centered on the hardships in getting a contract and on the processing of that contract on the Mexican side, sources of irritation in the United States included those related to nutrition (quality, quantity, type and time food was served), medical services, and lack of work.

In the early stages of the recruitment of Mexican laborers to the United States (1940s) there were enough jobs in the United States for those who applied. In the latter stages of the program (1950s and 1960s), however, work dried up because of the U.S. manpower released after World War II. That factor, coupled with Mexico's cycle of extreme dry weather and a cattle disease epidemic, left a large number of Mexican peasants without work. It was estimated that there were three million peasants desperate for jobs, therefore the rush and competition for getting to the United States was intense. For every job available, there were literally hundreds of Mexicans clamoring for it. The results were corruption, graft, and, in general, the bracero suffering extreme hardships in getting a contract. This aspect, however, was hardly touched on by the novelists. The novels concentrated on the negative aspects encountered by the braceros in the United States and neglected those found in Mexico. The bracero, to the contrary, was more aware, and possibly more hurt, by the treatment given to him by his own people.

An aspect completely neglected in the works of fiction was the pleasant experiences that the bracero actually had in the United States. Most of the braceros at one time or another reported a close, warm relationship formed with both farmers and Chicanos.

Another very important gain made by the bracero in his trip which was completely ignored by Mexican fiction writers, except Agustín Yáñez, was the geographic, social, political, and cultural education of the Mexican workers. Braceros became aware of the fact that the world was larger than a tiny village. They traveled to different parts of their own country, to Mexico City, or to their local state capitals to obtain the proper documents needed to go into the United States. They traveled to the border towns in Mexico: Reynosa, Matamoros, Piedras Negras, Juárez, Empalme, Mexicali, Tijuana. They became acquainted not only with Mexico

---

[1] "Coyote's Bite" (1955:36).

and its geography but with a foreign country that possessed different cultural traits. The Mexican peasants were very much aware of this extension of their horizon. All of them stated their awe, their pride, their satisfaction in learning and traveling to a strange and powerful country—and surprise, too, at the cultural diversity of Mexico itself.

By coming in contact with the different bureaucracies and the various documents necessary in the process of moving from one country to another, the braceros I interviewed had come to realize the importance of being able to read and write, of obtaining an education. His skills in reading and writing were constantly being put to the test either to sign documents or simply to write a letter back home. Therefore, the braceros interviewed were very proud of the fact that their children were receiving a much better education than they had had.

The majority of the Mexican fiction writers treated here did not know their braceros in depth. In seeking to present an intolerable situation and wishing to raise their voices against the existing conditions, the authors went to extremes. The bracero was and continues to be an embarrassment to the Mexican intellectual.

In summarizing the bracero experience, Pedro's story reminds us in the bracero's own words of what the experience has meant to the United States as well as to Mexico. With regard to the question of prejudice, the braceros I interviewed in Huecorio either were oblivious to prejudice that the Anglo-Saxon segment of the U.S. population might have directed at them or unconsciously repressed the idea altogether. Perhaps their isolation on American farms prevented them from interacting with the general population, and thus they did not come in contact with unpleasant racial experiences. Most braceros interviewed seemed to think Americans in general were fair and honest. Two of the sixteen braceros interviewed reported seeing ill-treatment by immigration officers, both episodes having taken place in Texas. Some braceros voiced complaints against Mexican-Americans who desired to prove their "Americaness" and who rejected their own past. These complaints did not embrace all Mexican-Americans, for close friendships had developed between the two groups. The friction between braceros and Mexican-Americans stemmed partly from the fact that Mexican-Americans were put in supervisory positions and were thus in charge of disciplining the braceros. Also contributing to this friction was the fact that Mexican-Americans saw their jobs threatened by the influx of cheap labor. The oversupply of labor kept wages at a minimum. To the bracero who took his savings home to Mexico where the rate of exchange was 12.50 pesos to 1 dollar, the wage rate paid by American farmers, even though it may have been low by American standards, was not viewed as such by the recipient. Not versed in economics or accustomed to the higher U.S. standard of living, he could not foresee the detrimental effects that such large numbers of Mexican workers had on the native American farmhand. Regardless of how the Mexican worker has been received in the U.S. countryside since the official end of the bracero program in 1964, he will continue to cross the border. He will go to any lengths to improve his standard of living. In desperation, all else having failed, and finding no source of employment or livelihood in his native land, he will go through any hardship in order to feed his family. As long as Mexican workers come home with radios, cars, clothing, and dollars, there will be a constant stream of them trekking to the United States. This was true for 1909 and is true for 1979. The "problem" is still with us. Until Mexico can provide adequate employment for its jobless, its destitute campesinos, braceros will continue to be part of the United States–Mexican scene whether in the form of "wetbacks" or "wire jumpers."

In sum the bracero folklore in Pedro's story has not been overcome by the elitelore in fiction about bracero life. That neither their folklore nor elitelore gives a complete picture is shown in the bracero folk song which brings together a wide body of lore to show the dimensions of the bracero experience. But the various types of folk song and the narrow scope in each prevent it from yielding a detailed portrait of bracero life. It is fair to conclude that there is no "single truth," but that the various lores about the bracero experience help us to better understand not only the lives of individuals as they move across national borders but also the needs of two nations that at once benefit from and endure the process.

Bibliography

Acosta, Oscar Zeta
  1973   *The Revolt of the Cockroach People.* San Francisco: Straight Arrow Books.
Almanza, Héctor Raúl
  1950   *Huelga blanca.* México: Academia Potosina de Artes y Ciencias.
Anaya, Rudolfo
  1972   *Bless Me, Ultima.* Berkeley: Tonatiuh International.
Anderson, Henry P.
  1960   "The Bracero Program in California." Berkeley: University of California School of Public Health; Mimeographed.
"Another Extension; Importation of Mexican Workers"
  1953   *Commonweal,* 79:213.
Armenta, Jesús
  n.d.   "El corrido de los mojados." *Cantares y estrellas.* México: Publicaciones ESCO, no. 32.
"Asparagus Aspersions: Dispute over Employment of Domestic or Foreign Workers"
  1965   *Newsweek,* 65:34.
"Battle over the Braceros in California"
  1965   *Business Week,* 9:24.
Becerra González, J. de Jesús
  1954   *El dólar viene del norte.* Guadalajara: México: Gráfica Editorial.
Belshaw, Michael
  1967   *A Village Economy: Land and People of Huecorio.* New York: Columbia University Press.
Brushwood, John Stubbs
  1966   *Mexico in Its Novel: A Nation's Search for Identity.* Austin: University of Texas Press.
Brushwood, John Stubbs, and José Rejas Gareidueñas
  1959   *Breve historia de la novela mexicana.* Madrid: Andrea.
Bustillo Oro, Juan
  1933   "Los que vuelven." *Tres dramas mexicanos.* México: Editorial Cenit.
Callejas, Julián
  1972   *Corridos mexicanos.* México: El Libro Español.

Campa, Arthur L.
　　1946　*Spanish Folk-Poetry in New Mexico.* Albuquerque, N.M.
Cardozo-Freeman, Inez
　　1976　"The Corridos of Arnulfo Castillo." *Revista Chicano-Riqueña,*
　　　　　4, 4:129–138.
Castellano, Rosario
　　1964　"La novela mexicana contemporánea y su valor testimonial."
　　　　　Hispania, 47:223–230.
Chavarri, Raúl
　　1964　"La novela moderna mejicana." *Cuadernos Hispanoamericanos,*
　　　　　58:367–378.
Colorado Legislative Council Committee on Migratory Labor
　　1960　*Migratory Labor in Colorado.* Research Publication No. 43,
　　　　　Denver.
"Coyote's Bite"
　　1955　*Time,* 65:36.
Díaz-Lastra, Alberto
　　1965　Carlos Fuentes y la revolución traicionada." *Cuadernos Hispa-*
　　　　　noamericanos, 62:369–375.
Eagleton, Terry
　　1976　*Marxism and Literary Criticism.* Berkeley and Los Angeles: Uni-
　　　　　versity of California Press.
Eckels, Richard P.
　　1954　"Hungry Workers, Ripe Crops, and the Non-Existent Mexi-
　　　　　can Border." *Reporter,* 10:28–32.
"Effects of Ending Bracero Program"
　　1967　*America,* 116:546.
Eldridge, Frank
　　1957　"Helping Hands from Mexico." *Saturday Evening Post,* 230:
　　　　　28–29.
"End of Bracero Program"
　　1963　*America,* 108:878–879.
"End Run on Braceros into the 20th Century"
　　1964　*America,* 111:791.
"Expiring Legislation"
　　1964　*Congressional Quarterly,* 22:30.
"Extension of Migrant Labor Agreement with Mexico"
　　1954　*U.S. Department of State Bulletin,* 30:53.
Flasher, John J.
　　1969　*México contemporáneo en las novelas de Agustín Yáñez.* México:
　　　　　Editorial Porrúa.
Foster, George M.
　　1967　*Tzintzuntzan.* Boston: Little Brown and Company.

Fuentes, Carlos
  1958 *La región más transparente.* México: Fondo de Cultura Económica.
  1960 *Where the Air Is Clear.* Trans. Sam. Hileman. New York: Ivan Obolensky.
  1969 *La nueva novela hispanoamericana.* México: Joaquín Mortiz.
Fuller, Varden
  1956 "Domestic and Imported Workers in the Harvest Labor Market." Santa Clara County, Calif. Report No. 184. Mimeographed.
Galarza, Ernesto
  1957 "Strangers in Our Field." *New Republic,* 136:18–19.
  1964 *Merchants of Labor.* Charlotte: McNally.
Gamio, Manuel
  1971 *The Life Story of the Mexican Immigrant.* New York: Dover Publications.
González, Manuel Pedro
  1951 *Trayectoria de la novela en México.* México: Ediciones Botas.
  1960 "Luis Spota, gran novelista en potencia." *Revista Hispánica Moderna,* 26:102–106.
González Navarro, Moisés
  1954 "Los braceros en el Porfiriato." *Estudios Sociológicos,* 2:261.
Goot, Donald
  1949 "Employment of Foreign Workers in United States Agriculture." *U.S. Department of State Bulletin,* 21:43–46.
Gordon, Donald K.
  1967 "Juan Rulfo, cuentista." *Cuadernos Americanos,* 155:198–208.
"Green Light for Braceros; Public Law 78."
  1961 *America,* 105:359.
Groom, P.
  1965 "Report from the National Farm Labor Conference." *Monthly Labor Report,* 88:275–278.
"Growers Face Loss of Braceros"
  1964 *Business Week,* 8:120.
Guerrero, Eduardo
  1924 *Canciones y corridos populares.* México: Eduardo Guerrero.
  1931 *Corridos históricos de la Revolución Mexicana desde 1910 a 1930 y otros notables de varias épocas.* México: Eduardo Guerrero, Editor.
Haddad, Elaine
  1964 "The Structure of *Al filo del Agua.*" *Hispania,* 47:522–529.
Hancock, Richard Humphris
  1959a *The Role of the Bracero in the Economic and Cultural Dynamics of Mexico: A Case Study of Chihuahua.* Ann Arbor, Michigan: University Microfilms.

1959*b*   *The Role of the Bracero in the Economic and Cultural Dynamics of Mexico: A Case Study of Chihuahua.* Stanford: Hispanic American Society.

Harss, Luis
  1966   "Juan Rulfo, Contemporary Mexican Novelist." *New Mexico Quarterly,* 35:293–318.
  1967   "Carlos Fuentes, Mexico's Metropolitan Eye." *New Mexico Quarterly,* 36:26–55.

Henestrosa, Andrés
  1977   *Espuma y flor de corridos mexicanos.* México: Editorial Porrúa.

Herrera, María Díaz
  1971   "The Bracero Experience: In Life and in Fiction." Master's thesis, UCLA Latin American Center, University of California, Los Angeles.
  1975   *See* Sobek, María Herrera.

Hill, Diane E.
  1968   "Integración, desintegración e intensificación en los cuentos de Juan Rulfo." *Revista Iberoamericana,* 34:331–338.

Hoffman, Abraham
  1976   *Unwanted Mexican Americans in the Great Depression.* Tucson: University of Arizona Press.

Irby, James East
  1956   *La influencia de William Faulkner en cuatro narradores hispanoamericanos.* México: Universidad Nacional Autónoma de México, Escuela de Verano.

Langle, Arturo
  1966   *Vocabulario; a todos, seudónimos, sobrenombres y hemerografía de la Revolución.* México: Universidad Nacional Autónoma de México, Instituto de Investigaciones Históricas.

Ledit, J. H.
  1947   "Cattle Plague in Mexico." *America,* 77:351–352.

León, Gamio C.
  1961   "Braceros Bring Home New Ways." *Americas,* 12:28–30.

Lewis, Oscar
  1961   *The Children of Sánchez.* New York: Random House.

McWilliams, Cary
  1943   "They Saved the Crops: Experiment in Planned Migration by Agreement between Mexico and the United States." *Inter American,* 2:10–14.

Mead, Robert G., Jr.
  1959   "Carlos Fuentes, Mexico's Angry Novelist." *Books Abroad,* 38:380–382.
  1966   "Literatura y política: imágenes iberoamericanas de los Estados Unidos." *Cuadernos Americanos,* 157:4.

1967   "Carlos Fuentes, airado novelista mexicano." *Hispania*, 50: 229–235.

Melo de Remes, María Luisa
1955a   "Brazos que se van." In *Brazos que se van*. México: Editorial Cultural. Pp. 13–19.
1955b   "Pobre patria mía." In *Brazos que se van*. México: Editorial Cultural. Pp. 175–178.

Mendoza, Vicente T.
1939   *El romance español y el corrido mexicano*. México: Ediciones de la Universidad Nacional Autónoma.
1961   "Paso del Norte." In *La canción mexicana*. Mexico: Instituto de Investigaciones Estéticas, Universidad Nacional Autónoma de México. Pp. 207–208.
1964   *Lírica narrativa de México: el corrido*. México: Instituto de Investigaciones Estéticas, Universidad Nacional Autónoma de México.

"Mexican Farm Labor"
1963a   *Congressional Quarterly*, 21:4.
1963b   *Congressional Quarterly*, 21:572–573.
1964   *Congressional Quarterly*, 22:9–10.

"Migrant Labor Agreement with Mexico"
1951   *U.S. Department of State Bulletin*, 25:336.

"Migratory Farm Labor"
1965   *Congressional Quarterly*, 23:634–635.

Mondragón, Magdalena
1956   *Tenemos sed*. México: Revista Mexicana de Cultura.

Monthly Review
1963   *Whither Latin America?* New York: Monthly Review Press.

Moore, Truman E.
1965   *The Slaves We Rent*. New York: Random House.

Muñoz, Rafael F.
1960   "El repatriado." In *Fuego en el norte*. México: Libro México Editores. Pp. 161–175.

Nelson, Eugene
1975   *Pablo Cruz and the American Dream: The Experiences of an Undocumented Immigrant from Mexico*. Layton, Utah: Peregrine Smith.

"Old Myth Fades: Bracero Program Ends in California"
1965   *Nation*, 201:31.

Ortega, Martínez Fidel
1969   *Carlos Fuentes y la realidad de México*. México: Tesis de Licenciatura en letras españolas, Universidad Iberoamericana.

Paredes, Américo
1966   "El folklore de los grupos de origen mexicano en Estados Unidos," *Folklore Americano*, 15:146–163.

1976   *A Texas-Mexican Cancionero: Folksongs of the Lower Border.* Urbana: University of Illinois Press.

Paz, Octavio
1969   *El laberinto de la soledad.* México: Fondo de Cultura Económica.

Rasmussen, Wayne D.
1951   *A History of the Emergency Farm Labor Supply Program.* Agriculture Monograph No. 13. Washington, D.C.: U.S. Department of Agriculture.

Real Academia Española
1939   *Diccionario de la lengua española.* Madrid. Talleres Espasa-Calpe.

Robles, Humberto J.
1970   "Los desarraigados." In Antonio Magaña-Esquivel, ed., *Teatro mexicano del siglo XX.* México: Fondo de Cultura Económica. Pp. 7–198.

Rodríguez-Alcalá, Hugo
1965   "Análisis estilístico de *El llano en llamas* de Juan Rulfo." *Cuadernos Americanos,* 140:211–234.

Rodríguez-Puértolas, Julio
1975   "La problemática socio-política chicana en corridos y canciones." *Aztlán* 6(1):97–116.

Rulfo, Juan
1953   "Paso del norte." In *El llano en llamas.* México: Fondo de Cultura Económica. Pp. 141–150.
1967   "Paso del norte." In *The Burning Plain and Other Stories.* Trans. George D. Schade. Austin: University of Texas Press. Pp. 147–156.

Samora, Julian
1971   *Los Mojados: The Wetback Story.* Notre Dame: University of Notre Dame Press.

Santamaría, Francisco J.
1942   *Diccionario general de americanismos.* Vol.· II. México: Editorial Pedro Robredo.

Scholes, Robert
1966   *Approaches to the Novel.* San Francisco: Chandler Publishing.

Schrieke, Bertram Johannes Otto
1936   *Alien Americans.* New York: The Viking Press.

Schwartz, Harry
1945   *Seasonal Farm Labor in the United States.* New York: Columbia University Press.

"Senate Committee Takes Up Immigration Law Revision"
1964   *Congressional Quarterly,* 22:113–114.

Shotwell, Louisa R.
1961   *The Harvesters.* New York: Doubleday.

Simmons, Merle E.
 1953   "Attitudes toward the United States Revealed in Mexican Co-
         rridos." *Hispania,* 361:34–42.
 1957   *The Mexican Corrido as a Source for Interpretative Study of Modern
         Mexico (1870–1950).* Indiana University Publications, Human-
         ities Series, 38. Bloomington: Indiana University Press.
Sobek, María Herrera
 1975   "The Function of Folklore in Gabriel García Márquez." Ph.D.
         dissertation, Spanish and Portuguese Department, University
         of California, Los Angeles.
Sommers, Joseph
 1966   "The Present Moment in the Mexican Novel." *Books Abroad,*
         40:261–266.
Soto, Antonio
 1959   "Bracero Story." *Commonweal,* 71:258–260.
Spota, Luis
 1948   *Murieron a mitad del río.* México: Talleres Gráficos de la Nación.
Taylor, Paul S.
 1932   "Songs of the Mexican Migration." *Texas Folklore Society,* 12:221–245.
Texas Legislative Council
 1956   *Transportation of Migrant Labor in Texas.* A Report to the 55th
         Legislature. Austin.
Tomasek, Robert Dennis
 1958   *The Political and Economic Implication of Mexican Labor under the
         Non Quota System, Contract Labor Program, and Wetback Movement.*
         Ann Arbor, Michigan: University Microfilms.
Topete, Jesús
 1949   *Aventuras de un bracero.* México: Editorial AmeXica.
United States Committee on Agriculture
 1958   *Hearings on Mexican Labor.* Washington, D.C.
United States Executive Agreement Series 278
 1943   *Temporary Migration of Mexican Agricultural Workers.* Washington,
         D.C.: Government Printing Office.
"U.S. and Mexican Agreement on Migratory Workers"
 1955   *U.S. Department of State Bulletin,* 32:701.
"U.S. and Mexico Sign Agricultural Workers Agreement."
 1949   *U.S. Department of State Bulletin,* 21:313–314.
Valdez, Luis, and Stan Steiner
 1972   "Corridos: The Songs of Exodus." In *Aztlan: An Anthology of
         Mexican Literature.* New York: Alfred A. Knopf. Pp. 132–137.
Vásquez Amaral, José
 1965   "La novelística de Agustín Yáñez." *Cuadernos Americanos,* 138:
         218–239.

Velasco Valdés, Miguel
   1967   *Repertorio de voces populares en México.* México: B. Costa-Amic., Editores México.
Villarreal, José Antonio
   1959   *Pocho.* Garden City, New York: Doubleday.
Wellek, Rene, and Warren Austin
   1956   *Theory of Literature.* New York: Harcourt, Brace & World.
"When U.S. Barred Foreign Workers from Farms: Bracero Ban"
   1965   *U.S. News,* 58:73–75.
"Who'll Pick the Strawberries: Problem of Braceros, Minimum Wages and Immigration Laws"
   1965   *Time,* 85:19.
Wilkie, James W.
   1973   *Elitelore.* Los Angeles: UCLA Latin American Center Publications, University of California.
Wilkie, James W., María Herrera-Sobek, and Edna Monzón de Wilkie
   1978   "Elitelore and Folklore: Theory and a Test Case in *One Hundred Years of Solitude,*" *Journal of Latin American Lore,* 4:183–224.
Wilkie, James W., and Edna Monzón de Wilkie
   1969   *México visto en el siglo XX: Entrevistas de historia oral con Ramón Betèta, Marte R. Gómez, Manuel Gómez Morín, Vicente Lombardo Toledano, Miguel Palomar y Vizcarra, Emilio Portes Gil, Jesús Silva Herzog.* México: Instituto Mexicano de Investigaciones Económicas.
Woodbridge, H. C.
   1945   "Mexico and U.S. Racisms: How Mexicans View Our Treatment of Minorities." *Commonweal,* 42:234–237.
Yáñez, Agustín
   1955   *Al filo del agua.* México: Editorial Porrúa. First ed., 1947.
   1963   *The Edge of the Storm.* Trans. Ethel Brinton. Austin: University of Texas Press.
Zerolo, E., M. de Toro, and E. Isaga
   1911   *Diccionario de la lengua castellana.* Paris: Casa Editorial Garnier Hermanos.

Discography

Ajua con "El Piporro"
> Eulalio González. Gas Records 4081.

Los alambrados
> Los Bukis. Mericana Records MM 6625.

A lo Piporro
> Eulalio González. Discos Musart TEDM 10656.

Cruzando el puente
> Los Cadetes de Linares. Ramex LP 1014.

De México a Laredo
> Dueto América. Caliente CLT 7242.

Lo mejor del Piporro
> Eulalio González. Discos Musart DC 787.

La muerte de un gallero
> Antonio Aguilar. Discos Musart ED-1721.

Soy inocente
> Antonio Aguilar. Discos Musart EDM 1700.

Las voces de los campesinos
> Francisco García and Pablo and Juanita Saludado. FM SC-1.

Index

140INDEX